# EISENHOWER

# EISENHOWER

## A Centennial Life

### WITH TEXT BY MICHAEL R. BESCHLOSS

PHOTOGRAPHS EDITED BY VINCENT VIRGA

An Edward Burlingame Book
*An Imprint of* HarperCollins*Publishers*

FIRST EDITION

DESIGNED BY JOEL AVIROM

Library of Congress Cataloging-in-Publication Data
Beschloss, Michael R.
Eisenhower: a centennial life/with text by Michael R. Beschloss;
photo editor, Vincent Virga; designer, Joel Avirom.—1st ed.
p.   cm.
Includes bibliographical references and index.
ISBN 0-06-016418-2
1.  Eisenhower, Dwight D. (Dwight David), 1890–1969—Pictorial
works.   2.  Presidents—United States—Pictorial
works.   3.  Generals—United States—Pictorial works.   I.  Virga,
Vincent.   II.  Title.
E836.B48   1990          89-46225
973.921′092—dc20
[B]

90  91  92  93  94   DT/CW   10  9  8  7  6  5  4  3  2  1

Quality Printing by Courier Company Inc.

# CONTENTS

# EISENHOWER

# 1.
# "CHANCE ARRANGEMENT OF FATE"

The white clapboard boyhood home in Abilene, Kansas, is now a shrine. A century after Dwight David Eisenhower's birth, the horses, chickens, ducks, pigs, rabbits, and nearby houses of the same austere design have been taken away. The clapboard house is surrounded now by monuments—the stone museum built after his Supreme Command, the stone library built after his Presidency, the stone chapel where he lies buried.

In the 1870s, this was a rakish neighborhood called the "Devil's Addition." For six years, Abilene was the culmination of the Chisholm Trail, capital of the Wild West where Hell was "in session," a town of gambling dens, saloons, and bordellos peopled by cowboys, cardsharps, gunslingers, and Wild Bill Hickok, who served as marshal. Then the trail moved on. Abilene once again became a sleepy congregation of four thousand souls, insular, Protestant, conservative, Republican, living off the rich farmland along the muddy river.

In 1878, excited by promotional pamphlets on Kansas as a New Eden of cheap, fertile land, his River Brethren grandparents, Jacob and Rebecca Eisenhower, sold their Pennsylvania farm for $8,500, rode here with their children on the Union Pacific Railroad, and bought a new acreage near Abilene for one-seventh the price of the old farm. When their son David married a college classmate, Ida Stover, in 1885, they gave him a dowry of $2,000 and 160 acres.

Shirking the farm life of his forebears and their pacifist, fundamentalist religion, David mortgaged the land and joined a partner to buy a general store in the nearby hamlet of Hope. In the 1888 farm depression, the store went bankrupt. The partner evidently fled, leaving David to face their creditors alone. The Eisenhowers lost everything but their clothes, a few household goods, and Ida's ebony piano.

On October 14, 1890, their third son, Dwight, was born in Denison, Texas, where David had found work as a ten-dollar-a-week railroad hand. The following year, his brother-in-law offered him mechanic's work at the Belle Springs Creamery in Abilene. He and Ida

Eisenhower's boyhood home as shrine. Opened to the public after World War II, it was a symbol of his advantage while running for President in 1952: What other presidential candidate's home was already a national monument?

Dwight *(left)* and brothers Edgar, Paul (who died in infancy), Roy, and Arthur. 1895.

brought their three sons home and took up residence in a shanty. Lacking money for a crib, they installed the new baby in an open bureau drawer. In 1898, David's veterinarian brother, Abraham Lincoln Eisenhower, offered him his much larger white clapboard house near the railroad tracks for a nominal rent on condition that he take care of their father. David agreed and moved his family into the home that now stands as the monument in Abilene. Fifty years later, the third son observed that even this larger house had less floor space than his office at the Pentagon.

As Dwight and his five brothers matured, the parents did not shield them from their experience of financial ruin. David channelled part of his rage into a general hatred of lawyers, complaining that the man he had hired to sell off his store and pay his debts had stolen what few dollars remained. Years later, shortly before he died, he told his eldest son, Edgar, "I got something that has bothered me for a long time. I am not going to leave you boys anything. That breaks my heart." As Edgar recalled, "Dad cried, the first time I ever saw him cry in his life."

Normally soft-spoken, Ida endlessly warned her sons against "thieves, embezzlers, chiselers, and all kinds of crooks." Told the tale over and over again, a boy other than the young Eisenhower might have been driven to radical action against the system of businessmen, bankers, and lawyers that had devastated his family. Dwight's attitude toward the establishment of Abilene and points east was not to beat them but join them. Like his martinet father, and in response to him, he had a volatile temper. Ida told him that in conquering it, he had "the most to learn" of all her boys. Many years later, a friend observed that were Eisenhower not so practiced at directing his emotions into his work, his intense "unloosened energy" and "great emotional potentiality" might have made him "unbalanced."

On Halloween 1900, told that he was too young to go out with his older brothers, Dwight pounded a tree with bleeding fists until David beat him with a hickory switch and sent him to bed, sobbing, feeling "hurt, completely abused and at odds with the entire world," as the son later recalled. Ida came into the bedroom and said, "He who con-

18

The Abilene of Eisenhower's youth (below left).

Dwight (called "Little Ike" by schoolmates), Edgar ("Big Ike"), Arthur, Earl, and Roy stand in rear. Ida and David Eisenhower sit in front, with Milton in the center.

quereth his own soul is greater than he who taketh a city." She noted that the object of his anger probably didn't care, possibly didn't even know, and thus the only person injured was himself. In 1967, Eisenhower remembered this as "one of the most valuable moments of my life. . . . To this day I make it a practice to avoid hating anyone. If someone's been guilty of despicable actions, especially toward me, I try to forget him."

He later said that his boyhood was so much fun that he never knew he was poor. But Edgar recalled that when he and Dwight peddled the family's produce to more affluent families in town, "they'd make us feel like beggars": "It made us scrappers. Any time anybody walked on us, they heard from us." The father did not disapprove. Once when Dwight ran home from a boy who wanted to fight, David told him to go back and stand up for his rights.

Mornings and evenings the parents led the sons in Scripture reading, passing a great Bible from hand to hand. "I never heard a cross word between them," said Dwight many years later. "Before their children, they were not demonstrative in their love for each other, but a quiet, mutual devotion permeated our home." Eisenhower said that "ambition without arrogance was quietly instilled by both my parents. Whenever any of us expressed a wish for something that seemed far beyond our reach, my mother often said, 'Sink or swim' or 'Survive or perish.'" The parents proclaimed, "Opportunity is all around you. Reach out and take it."

Their influence was undeniably effective. From the household of six boys (the seventh died in infancy) came six accomplished men—a university president, a lawyer, a druggist, a banker, a businessman, and the soldier who became General of the Army and President of the United States. Eisenhower later recalled that his father's lifelong ambition was to "get to the place where he could look without pain" at his business failure and "to be quite a material success. But then he got so interested in his boys and in seeing them occupy prominent positions in life."

Eisenhower matured with a robust, almost swaggering self-confidence. As an Abilene High School student, he "frankly idolized"

Dwight *(second boy from left in front row)* and others in Miss Addie B. Over's seventh-grade class. He later said that his boyhood was so much fun he never knew his family was poor, but an Abilene friend observed, "Surely it must have been difficult, even humiliating for him, wearing his mother's high-buttoned shoes to school." 1902–03.

Eisenhower on the Abilene High School baseball team. In early 1905, told that his leg might have to be amputated to overcome blood poisoning, he said, "I'd rather be dead than crippled and not be able to play ball," and made his brother Edgar promise to make sure that "under no circumstances" would the operation be performed. Other measures stopped the illness. The story later became a central tale in the Eisenhower lore, demonstrating the steely will of the national hero-to-be, as well as the fact that his decisions on D-Day 1944 were not the first time the General made a high-stakes gamble and won.

George Washington—his "stamina and patience," his modesty, "courage, daring and capacity for self-sacrifice." He loved to camp and fish, but his grand passion was baseball and football: "I could not imagine an existence in which I was not playing one or both." Once when teammates learned that the center of a visiting football team was black and said they would not play across the line from him, Eisenhower replied that he would play center that day—not out of any preternatural instinct for civil rights but for reasons of civility and fair play. He shook hands with his black opponent and later wrote in his journal, "Rest of the team was a bit ashamed."

After high school graduation in 1909, he planned to follow Edgar to the University of Michigan. Before going to Ann Arbor, he would work in the creamery for a year or two to help Edgar financially. Then Edgar would drop out to let him have his start. Dwight's closest friend, Swede Hazlett, son of an Abilene doctor, urged him to apply to join him at the Naval Academy. Annapolis promised a free education, but schooling for war delighted the senior Eisenhowers no more than Edgar's ambition to become a lawyer. Too old for Annapolis, Dwight bid for and won a merit appointment to West Point. In June 1911, unwilling to "look a gift horse in the mouth," he went to the Abilene station and boarded an eastbound train. Ida retired to her room, the first time her youngest son, Milton, heard his mother cry.

Isolated, complacent, composed mainly of white rural Protestants like Eisenhower, West Point in 1911 was anything but a place of ferment. Cadets rode horses, pitched tents for the summer at the far end of the famous Plain, and studied geology, mathematics, natural philosophy, engineering, and hygiene through rote methods little altered since the War of 1812. The opposite of civilian schools that specialized in stripping late adolescents of their certitudes, West Point instilled belief in the importance of the team over the individual, the unperfectability of man, the self-interest of civilians and, as one teacher put it, the preeminence of the President of the United States over "mere politicians and their dishonest principles of action."

Eisenhower drilled himself to become what one sportswriter called "one of the most promising backs in Eastern football." Just before the Army-Navy game of 1912, he badly injured his knee. A West Point doctor told him that his career in team sports was over. This news plunged him into a funk that lasted two years: "I was almost despondent and several times had to be prevented from resigning. Life seemed to have little meaning. A need to excel was gone."

Robbed of the principal source of his self-esteem and the primary outlet for his great energy, he began smoking, despite frequent demerits, and took up poker. His grades fell. He insulted a Plebe with uncharacteristic viciousness and felt "stupid and unforgivable." He talked back to a teacher so insolently that he risked expulsion. When he stood at a local shooting gallery in street clothes, someone unaccountably called him "soldier boy": "For the first time in my life, a fit of trembling overcame me. My hands shook. Without a word, I laid down

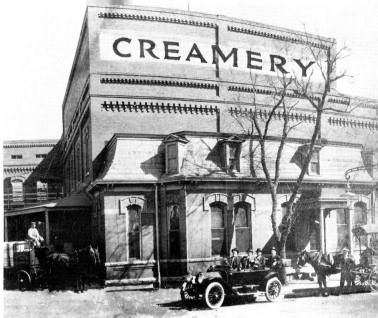

the rifle and left the place without a backward glance. Never before or since have I experienced the same kind of attack."

Eisenhower's emotional state was evinced in letters he sent in November 1913 to a close Abilene friend, Ruby Norman, who wrote him that her tour with a six-girl orchestra might bring her to New York during his Christmas leave. He replied that "if you go home, nothing can happen which will prevent us being just as good friends as always —and if you'd spend your vacation in N.Y., we don't know *what might* happen. . . . Fact is, I feel right devilish tonight, you know—just like I could smoke a cigarette, and swear and do all the other mean things like drinking pop. . . . At any rate I'm not going to open up and tell you all I'd really like to this evening. No thank you—I want to hear from you again."

He groused, "Seems like I'm never cheerful any more. The fellows that used to call me 'Sunny Jim' call me 'Gloomy Face' now. . . . I sure hate to be so helpless and worthless. . . . I'm getting to be such a confirmed grouch you'd hardly know me." He had "never had such a protracted case of the blue devils in my life. . . . The only bright spot is, just now, that trouble with Mexico seems imminent. . . . You know, I believe it would be great sport to play the leading role in one of these present day five cent (selling for a dollar and a half) novels— don't you? I'm not tall and graceful enough to be a Robert Chambers hero—nor big enough to be one of Jack London's. But just for an ordinary author, who is not too darn particular about his leading man —I might fill the place nicely. . . . I've changed my views concerning matrimony. I saw in the paper that it was 'kisstomary to cuss the bride' so me for it. I'm looking for someone that I can pummel and bruise and pinch and fight and etc etc."

The final straw came just before commencement in 1915. Told by West Point authorities that his bad knee might prohibit an Army career, he flippantly replied that it was all right with him. He sent away for information on life as an Argentine gaucho. Then his commission came through and he cast off his feigned indifference: In his second lieutenant's uniform, he paraded up and down the dusty streets of Abilene and more than once got drunk.

Eisenhower at West Point. His military career began with so little forethought that, he later wrote, "From the first day at West Point, and any number of times thereafter, I often asked myself: What am I doing here? . . . By what chance arrangement of fate did I come by this uniform?" 1911–15.

Abilene, Kansas.
March 25, 1911.

Sen. J. L. Bristow,
Salina, Kans.

Dear Sir:

Having learned from my parents, that you are again in Salina, I take this opportunity of thanking you for my appointment to West Point.

Although I wrote to you immediately after receiving the appointment last November, its value to me has been greatly increased, since I was notified that I had passed the entrance examinations. I took the examinations at Jefferson Barracks, Mo., in January.

One of my alternates, Mr. Platner, did not pass, but I understand the other one did.

I have been ordered to report at West Point, June 14, this year.

So trusting that you will accept my heartiest thanks for the great favor you have conferred upon me, I am

Respectfully Yours.
Dwight Eisenhower

Mamie Geneva Doud and her parents in San Antonio, Texas.

That summer, the last he ever spent in the town of his youth, he fell in love with Gladys Harding, the blond daughter of the owner of all of the freight business in Abilene. The father evidently warned her that the young man would not amount to anything. Eisenhower wrote her on August 18 that "more than ever now I want to hear you say the three words more than I ever have. . . . For, girl, I do love you and want you to *know* it. To be as certain of it as I am. To believe in me and trust in me as you do your dad."

A week later, he wrote that "your love is my whole world. Nothing else counts at all." After reading one of her letters, "my eyes filled with tears and I simply had to stop and whisper over and over I love you Gladys, I love you Gladys. And now my beautiful lady, I'm going to read your letter once more, then I'll meet you in dreamland, if you will meet me there. And there, as sometime in reality, you shall be my dearest and closest friend, my own sweetheart and true blue *wife*." Whether because of her father's opposition, her aversion to a life in the Army, or her ambition for a serious piano-playing career, Gladys put him off, citing her work.

He had longed for assignment to the Philippines. The Army sent him to Fort Sam Houston in San Antonio. Within a month he met Mamie Geneva Doud, the breezy, eighteen-year-old daughter of a well-to-do Denver meat packer who wintered with his family in San Antonio. Introduced to her as the "woman-hater of the post" (perhaps a result of the disappointment with Gladys), Eisenhower found the girl "saucy in the look about her face and in her whole attitude. If she had been intrigued by my reputation as a woman-hater, I was intrigued by her appearance."

By January 1916, he was writing Ruby Norman, "The girl I run around with is named Miss Doud, from Denver. . . . Pretty nice—but awful strong for society—which often bores me. But we get along well together—and I'm at her house whenever I'm off duty—whether it's morning—noon—night. Her mother and sisters are fine—and we have lots of fun together." Still smarting from his failed romance, he wrote that if she wished to know more about Miss Doud, he would be glad to oblige, "*since* [underlined twice] I learned that G. H. cared so terribly for her work." After an eight-month courtship of vaudeville evenings, river walks, and fifty-cent Mexican dinners, he and Mamie were married in July at the Doud home in Denver. Then he took his new wife by train to meet his family in Abilene. She cried, "At last I have some brothers!"

As Ruby Norman's daughter recalled, when Gladys Harding heard of the impending marriage, "she was furious" because "she thought Dwight was going to marry her. . . . She went on the train to Kansas City, and on the train was Cecil Brooks [a well-to-do Abilene widower]. He asked her to marry him, and she said yes. My mother told me this was to spite Dwight. . . . Gladys had to be married before Eisenhower, and she was—sixteen days before. . . . I always thought that Gladys didn't treat Cecil very well. When he died, she went into a total nervous breakdown. My mother . . . said this was guilt because she never really loved Cecil." Many years later, Gladys bound up Eisenhower's love letters along with a four-leaf clover and a faded rose and gave them to her son with a note: "Letters from Dwight Eisenhower when we were young and happy, 1914 and 1915. Not to be opened or published in any way whatsoever until after his death and Mamie's and also after my death."

Mamie recalled that when she met her husband-to-be, she was tired of "all those lounge lizards with patent leather hair." But she had also been a pampered girl who rarely wanted for anything. Now she had to make do on a starting officer's salary. While the senior Douds found Eisenhower trustworthy and likable, friends expressed their view that "Mamie could have done a good deal better" and that he was "marrying above his class."

The marriage was devoted but not always serene. Eisenhower was sometimes rattled by his wife's impulsiveness. In her last years, Mamie recalled, "Ike never told me what I should do because he knew I'd go right out and do the exact opposite." She joked that the "secret of our marriage" was the fact they had "absolutely nothing in common." She was sometimes unsettled by his emotional reticence and his temper. In 1960, Eisenhower's White House doctor recorded, "Mamie told me she had been jittery all night and did not sleep because the President had said something to her after his return from Georgia last evening

25

Miss Doud Weds
Lieutenant Eisenhower.

MR. AND MRS. JOHN SHELDON
Doud announce the marriage of their daughter, Mamie Geneva, to Lieutenant D. D. Eisenhower of the United States army stationed at Fort Sam Houston, Tex., which took place Saturday at high noon in their home at 705 Lafayette street.

Only relatives witnessed the impressive ceremony which was performed by the Rev. William Williamson of Leicester, England, who is now visiting in Denver and is a close friend of the bride's parents. An interesting feature of the ceremony was that it is the first time the

ANNOUNCEMENT.

Mr. and Mrs. John Sheldon Doud announce the marriage of their daughter, Mamie Geneva, to Lieutenant Dwight D. Eisenhower, United States Army, Saturday, July 1, at Denver.

Lieutenant and Mrs. Eisenhower are at home in their quarters, Fort Sam Houston, where Lieutenant Eisenhower is stationed with the Nineteenth Infantry. Mrs. Eisenhower will be remembered as Miss Doud, who has spent several winters here and has [be]en a popular member of the social set.

Brett & I.

Another fine example of modern Engi

Hoping it will hold.

Still holding his temporary wartime rank of lieutenant colonel, Eisenhower accompanied an Army truck convoy across the American continent. In his private album he mounted and annotated these pictures of the journey. 1919.

Some bridge!

The Eisenhowers and their first child, Doud Dwight— "Icky," born September 24, 1917. A half century after the boy's death in 1920, Mamie Eisenhower recalled, "It was as if a shining light had gone out in Ike's life. Throughout all the years that followed, the memory of those bleak days was a deep inner pain that never seemed to diminish much."

which cut her deeply." On another occasion, "Mamie and Ike sat around in the West Hall and got into some conversation about which Ike blew up in anger."

She hated the Army's lack of privacy, the constant moves to other posts, the frequent departures: "I never got used to him being gone. He was my husband. He was my whole life." She was unengrossed in the details of his career at a time when he was growing more earnest, accomplished, and preoccupied. Still, she fulfilled her roles with gaiety, charm, poise, and seriousness. He benefited from her judgments of people and her help in "smoothing the edges off the rough-and-ready Kansan," as their son later said, "teaching him some of the polish that later stood him in good stead." She accepted his priorities. "My country comes first," he once told her. "You come second."

In 1917, Mamie bore a son, Doud Dwight, whom they called "Icky." Intent on being the father David had never been, Eisenhower adored the child, for whom he made ludicrous faces, prowled on the floor as a kitten, and pranced as a clown. As the family moved from post to post, the boy was a favorite of the enlisted men. One recalled that Eisenhower planned to make him "one of the greatest soldiers of all time."

Then catastrophe. The son died at three of scarlet fever. Almost a half century later Eisenhower called it "the greatest disappointment and disaster in my life, the one I have never been able to forget completely." As President, spotting daffodils in the Oval Office, he noted to his secretary that yellow had been Icky's favorite color. The adored son's death, he later wrote, was "a tragedy from which we never recovered." He felt "on the ragged edges of a breakdown." Not long afterwards, his bid to enter infantry school at Fort Benning, Georgia, was rejected, dashing hopes for quick promotion. He considered quitting the Army.

The cheerful, spontaneous, almost carefree quality in Eisenhower's personality so evident in the Abilene boyhood had survived the end of his football career and the close brush with losing his commission. But this trauma put the iron in his soul. Some who knew him thought the disaster pushed him to absorb himself in his military career; others thought he would never again lose himself in another human being. Musing in his diary twenty-five years later on a friend's hardship, he wrote, "Makes one wonder whether any human ever dares become so wrapped up in another that all happiness and desire to live is determined by the actions, desires—or life—of the second."

The marriage could not have been unaffected by the ordeal. The parents reproached themselves over what could have been done to save the child. A friend of Mamie's thought they were "two young people who were drifting apart." In 1922, a second son, John Sheldon Doud, was born. As Eisenhower recalled, John "did much to fill the gap that we felt so poignantly and so deeply every day of our lives."

In the 1920s, even for a soldier lacking Eisenhower's ambition, energy, and will, the prospect of a lifetime in the Army was dismal.

Weary of war, Presidents and Congress cut troop strength to the bone. Men promoted during the world war were reduced to lower permanent ranks where they languished. During the war, Eisenhower had maneuvered to the point of official reprimand to win an overseas troop command. Instead he was ordered to train units in the United States before they went overseas. Finally he was assigned to go to France. One week before sailing, the Armistice was signed. Stripped of his wartime promotion to lieutenant colonel, he was once again a major.

In 1922 he went to Panama as executive officer under Brigadier General Fox Conner, an erudite Mississippian who had been wartime chief of operations under General Pershing. Forty years later, Eisenhower still called him "the ablest man I ever knew." Conner saw in Eisenhower the makings of a commander and enrolled him in his own one-man graduate school, assigning and cross-examining him on books from his rich library on politics, philosophy, dramatic poetry, military doctrine, and history, especially on the Civil War. The pupil later said that reading Clausewitz under Conner was the most important intellectual influence on his military career.

Eisenhower recalled that "one of the most profound beliefs of General Conner was that the world could not long avoid another major war. . . . Under conditions as they were he was quite certain that the Treaty of Versailles carried within it the seeds of another, larger conflagration. He urged me to be ready for it." Conner helped arrange an appointment to the Command and General Staff School at Fort Leavenworth, a vital passport to Army advancement, and told his protégé, "You are far better trained and ready for Leavenworth than anybody I know. . . . You will feel no sense of inferiority." Eisenhower finished first in his class, which he later considered "a watershed in my life."

What followed were orders to Fort Benning, "where I was supposed to command a battalion *and coach football*," then assignment to help write a guidebook for the United States Battle Monuments Commission, which exposed him to General Pershing and, fatefully, to the battlefields of France. Next he attended the Army War College in Washington, pinnacle of the Army's postgraduate education system.

John Sheldon Doud Eisenhower, named for Mamie's father, born in Denver on August 3, 1922.

29

Camp Gaillard, Panama: General Fox Conner awards a commission to Eisenhower, who later wrote that Conner was "the one more or less invisible figure to whom I owe an incalculable debt." 1922.

The Eisenhowers in San Remo and on the Rhine above Coblentz. 1929.

Milton Eisenhower was living in the Capital as an information officer for the Department of Agriculture. At a cocktail party, he collared a reporter and said, "Please don't go until you've met my brother. He's a major in the Army and I know he's going places." (The man looked at the brother, then in his late thirties, and said if he was, he had better start going soon.) The War College was followed by another tour with the Battle Monuments Commission, with Eisenhower tramping across the battlegrounds of France and Belgium.

In 1929, thirty-nine years old, he was appointed an aide to the assistant secretary of war in Washington. Almost ineluctably he was drawn into the orbit of the grandiloquent new Army Chief of Staff, General Douglas MacArthur. He respected MacArthur's mind ("a hell of an intellect—My God, but he was smart") and was entertained by his histrionics ("with that dramatic voice, he could have been a great actor"), but not always by the General's right-wing views and his penchant for publicizing them. Eisenhower was shocked at how MacArthur crossed the "clean-cut line between the military and the political" and how "my duties were beginning to verge on the political, even to the edge of partisan politics."

Drafting MacArthur's correspondence, statements, and reports, he drank in what he saw, kept his doubts to himself, and honed his skills in bureaucratic politics and attracting the favorable attention of influential superiors. Many years later, when a reporter noted that he did not seem to like the role of politician, Eisenhower replied, "What the hell are you talking about? I have been in politics, the most active sort of politics, most of my adult life. There's no more political organization in the world than the armed services of the U.S."

During these years, he was exposed to national issues at first hand. "While I have no definite leanings toward any political party," he wrote in his diary after Franklin Roosevelt's 1932 election, "I believe it is a good thing the Democrats won—and particularly that one party will have such overwhelming superiority in Congress. . . . Things are not going to take an upturn until more power is centered in one man's hands. Only in that way will confidence be inspired, will it be possible to do some of the obvious things for speeding recovery, and will we be freed from the pernicious influence of noisy and selfish minorities. For two years I have been called 'Dictator Ike' because I believe that virtual dictatorship must be exercised by our President, so now I keep still—but I still believe it!"

In 1935, he followed MacArthur to the Philippines, where President Manuel Quezon had secured the General's services as military adviser. Eisenhower thought "it would have been a wonderful experience, except for the lack of money. Everything we did was on a shoestring." The American mandate was to conceive defense of the islands, but Eisenhower soon concluded that Quezon's main desire was to build "a military adequate to deal with domestic revolt." Planning was undermined by corruption, low morale, and inadequate funding. Ensconced with Mamie in a suite at the Manila Hotel, Eisenhower entertained visiting American businessmen, played bridge with Quezon on his yacht, and sunbathed. He regained the rank of lieutenant colonel. His conflicts with MacArthur were growing more open and frequent.

In May 1936, he wrote in an occasional diary, "Jim [Major James B. Ord, who was working with Eisenhower on the Philippine defense plan] and I undertook to get the general to modify his order to call twenty thousand men next January . . . and he gave us one of his regular shouting tirades. He seemed particularly bitter toward me."

In September 1936, when Franklin Roosevelt was running for a second term against Alf Landon of Kansas, "TJ [Captain T. J. Davis, MacArthur's administrative aide] and I came in for a terrible bawling out. . . . The general has been following the *Literary Digest* poll and has convinced himself that Landon is to be elected, probably by a landslide. I showed him letters from Arthur Hurd [an Abilene lawyer and old friend], which predict that Landon cannot even carry Kansas, but he got perfectly furious when TJ and I counseled caution in studying the *Digest* report. We couldn't understand the reason for his almost hysterical condemnation of our stupidity until he suddenly let drop that he had gone out and urged Q[uezon] to shape his plans for going to the United States on the theory that Landon will be elected. . . . [W]hy should he get sore just because we say, 'Don't be so d— certain and go out on a limb unnecessarily.' Both of us 'are fearful and small-

July 1932: Twenty thousand Bonus Marchers, jobless veterans of World War I, come to Washington and camp along Pennsylvania Avenue to demand early payment on their promised 1945 bonus. Insisting that revolution is in the air, General MacArthur orders his unhappy aide Major Eisenhower to stand with him and watch Army units clear the men away. Eisenhower much later told an historian, "I told that dumb son-of-a-bitch he had no business going down there. I told him it was no place for the Chief of Staff."

31

Eisenhower in the Philippines, as his relations with MacArthur deteriorate. 1935–39.

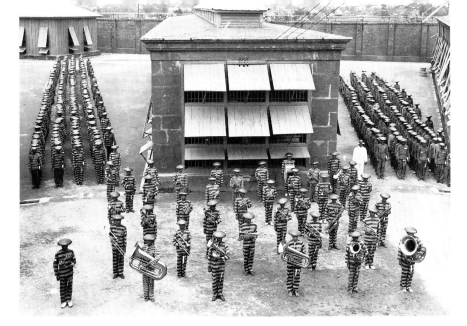

minded people who are afraid to express judgments that are obvious from the evidence at hand.' Oh hell.''

Despite Eisenhower's insistence that it was unaffordable, Mac-Arthur ordered him to hold a grand parade of troops in Manila. The perturbed Quezon asked who had given such a command. MacArthur denied that it was he. Eisenhower later exploded: "General, all you're saying is that I'm a liar, and I'm *not* a liar, and so I'd like to go back to the United States right away." MacArthur slung an arm over his shoulder and said, "Ike, it's just fun to see that damn Dutch temper take you over." Years later Eisenhower said, "Now, *that's* the time. From there on, our relationships were never really close."

He was almost fifty. Through the 1920s and 1930s, he had served with troops for a total of only six months. "During all those years," he later wrote a friend, "I was passed around from one general to another as one of the senior staff people and, in spite of my protests,

was never allowed to go to a troop position. . . . I was so anxious to get away from staff work and get into the field where a man could exercise some authority in his own little bailiwick and indulge in more physical activity than was possible behind the desk, that I frequently made myself objectionable to my bosses (never so much, however, that they would relieve me)."

He continued to ask for a troop command. Unknown to him, MacArthur blocked these requests in order to keep him. The Army personnel office told Eisenhower that an officer of his age and rank would probably not become a colonel until about 1950. Then he would be sixty, too old to become a general. "Happy in my work and ready to face, without resentment, the bleak promotional picture, I had long ago refused to bother my head about promotion," he later wrote. "Whenever the subject came up among the three of us at home, I said the real satisfaction was for a man who did the best he could."

These words contain the ring of one protesting too much. In September 1939, when war broke out in Europe, Eisenhower told MacArthur, "The United States cannot remain out of this war for long. I want to go home as soon as possible." The General told him he was making a mistake. President Quezon offered him anything to stay. But on the eve of 1940, the Eisenhowers left Manila by steamship, with MacArthur and his wife waving from the dock. Eisenhower wrote a friend that "we're going to fight, and no one is going to 'lead' us into it." Americans would not forever tolerate "such great expenditures in money, time, resources and effort" just to be prepared to meet the threat from Germany. Eventually public opinion would decide that it was cheaper to simply remove the threat: "The American population, once it gets truly irritated, is a self-confident, reckless, fast-moving avalanche . . . and it is *our* job to speed up the preparatory forces!"

After serving as Executive Officer of the Fifteenth Infantry and commanding a brigade in California, Eisenhower was appointed Chief of Staff of the Third Army, throwing him into the greatest peacetime military exercise in American history. Roughly 240,000 men of the Third Army were matched against 180,000 of the Second under battle conditions in Louisiana—"a God-awful spot . . . with mud, malaria, mosquitoes and misery." Eisenhower's strategic planning and leadership almost achieved capture of the Second Army's commander. Franklin Roosevelt, reading about the war games at the White House, was much impressed.

On December 7, 1941, now a brigadier general, Eisenhower was "dead tired" as he ate lunch: "My ambition was short-range. I wanted to capitalize on the Sunday afternoon and take a long nap." He told Mamie that he did not want to be "bothered by anyone wanting to play bridge." Awakened by the bulletin from Pearl Harbor, he was summoned to the War Department for emergency duty: "Hop a plane and get up here right away."

The Louisiana maneuvers, summer 1941: On the eve of World War II, Eisenhower conceives and directs strategy for the 240,000-man Third Army in an "invasion" of Lousiana, while the 180,000-man Second Army acts in "defense" of the United States. The Army Chief of Staff, General George Marshall, staged the vast war game to find flaws in training and equipment and quietly assess talent in the officer corps. During the game, Eisenhower lives in a tent in a bivouac near Lake Charles. In the *New York Times,* Hanson Baldwin observed that had the exercise been "real war," the Second Army "would have been annihilated."

# 2.
# NEITHER NAPOLEON NOR CAESAR

The sometimes drowsy look of the Manila years gave way to scenes of a man thrust into the role for which he had prepared all of his life, springing before dawn from a bed in his brother Milton's house outside Washington, barging into frenzied offices at the War Department, working around the clock, stopping only for a hot dog or a ham sandwich.

During the heartbreaking early weeks of the war, the legendary Army Chief of Staff, General George Marshall, complained, "It's hard as hell to find anybody in our high command who's worth a damn." When Eisenhower arrived in Marshall's office on Sunday morning, December 14, 1941, Marshall described the ordeal in the Pacific—the sunken ships at Pearl Harbor, the planes destroyed outside Manila, the other Japanese assaults—as well as troop strength in the Philippines and intelligence on other current and potential assets. He leaned across his desk and stared at Eisenhower: "What should be our general line of action?" The younger man paused and said, "Give me a few hours."

After dusk, he returned with pages of yellow tissue paper headed "Steps to Be Taken." He knew the Philippines were beyond saving, that the prudent course would be retreat to Australia to gird for coun-terattack. But this would ignore the need to renew American prestige in the Far East, not to mention the honor of the Army. He recom-mended expanding the Australian base: "We must take great risks and spend any amount of money re-quired." Still, Washington must do everything it could to save and bolster MacArthur's forces: Amer-ica's Pacific friends "may excuse failure but they will not excuse abandonment" of the islands.

Marshall agreed: "Do your best to save them." Placing Eisenhower immediately in charge of the Philippines and Far Eastern section of the War Plans Division, he said (with an eye that struck his visitor as "awfully cold"), "Eisenhower, the Department is filled with able men who analyze their problems well but feel compelled always to bring them to me for final solution. I must have assistants who will solve

The Japanese bomb Pearl Harbor *(opposite)* and the Philippines.

The Führer at his zenith. In his September 1939 diary, after the Nazis invaded Poland, Eisenhower had written of Adolf Hitler as "a power-drunk egocentric . . . one of the criminally insane. . . . Unless he is successful in overcoming the whole world by brute force, the final result will be that Germany will have to be dismembered."

June 1942 (opposite): Eisenhower arrives in England to form "the best army that the United States has ever put into the field." He writes a West Point classmate, "This is a long tough road we have to travel. . . . Fake reputations, habits of glib and clever speech, and glittering surface performance are going to be discovered and kicked overboard." Here, at a demonstration by British airborne troops, he is greeted by the British Secretary for Air, Sir Archibald Sinclair.

their own problems and tell me later what they have done."

Eisenhower worked without success to save the Philippines, leading MacArthur to heap the blame on him, along with Marshall and Roosevelt. Eisenhower confided his resentment to his diary: "Looks like MacArthur is losing his nerve. I'm hoping that his yelps are just his way of spurring us on, but he is always an uncertain factor." When MacArthur's outgunned and outnumbered American and Filipino forces held out for months on the Bataan Peninsula, Eisenhower wrote: "Bataan is made to order for him. It's in the public eye; it has made him a public hero; it has all the essentials of drama; and he is the acknowledged king on the spot." But "in a war such as this, when high command invariably involves a president, a prime minister, six chiefs of staff, and a horde of lesser 'planners,' there has got to be a lot of patience—no one person can be a Napoleon or a Caesar."

On March 10, 1942, "Father died this morning. Nothing I can do but send a wire." The next day: "I should like so much to be with my Mother these few days. But . . . war is not soft, it has no time to indulge even the deepest and most sacred emotions. . . . I'm quitting work now, 7:30 P.M. I haven't the heart to go on tonight." The next day: "I've shut off all business and visitors for thirty minutes, to have that much time, by myself, to think of him. . . . He was a just man, well liked, well educated, a thinker. He was undemonstrative, quiet, modest, and of exemplary habits—he never used alcohol or tobacco. He was an uncomplaining person in the face of adversity. . . . I'm proud he was my father. My only regret is that it was always so difficult to let him know the great depth of my affection for him."

Marshall found that Eisenhower lived up to his advance billing. He was the opposite of the kind of officers for whom Marshall had no use —self-seekers, self-publicists, pessimists, buck-passers, the flamboyant, men obsessed with detail. The two men were both admirers of Fox Conner, close students of the Civil War and other military history. Unlike Eisenhower, Marshall was an austere loner, but the younger man quickly regarded him with "affection" and "unlimited admiration and respect."

Marshall made Eisenhower his principal plans and operations officer as head of the War Plans Division, but aroused his ire by saying that unlike the last war, the field officers, not the staff officers, would now win the promotions: "I know that you were recommended by one general for division command. . . . I'm glad they have that opinion of you, but you are going to stay right here and fill your position, and that's that!" Seething at the notion of missing another war in order to sit in Washington, Eisenhower said he would do his duty: "If that locks me to a desk for the rest of the war, so be it!" He filled a page of his diary with angry words against Marshall for toying with him, and then tore it out: "Anger cannot win, it cannot even think clearly."

His worry about never commanding troops was short-lived. Marshall recommended his promotion to major general (temporary). Delighted, Eisenhower wrote, "This should assure that when I finally get

back to troops, I'll get a division." With Eisenhower at its head, War Plans was folded into a new Operations Division to oversee Army activities all over the world. This gave him responsibility for grand strategy and a sense of the sweep of modern war.

London and Washington had to agree on what to do in the European theater in 1942. Eisenhower had at first supported going all out in the Pacific, but his exposure to the views of Marshall and British officers in Washington helped to move him toward a program of putting Germany first. This meant keeping the Soviet Union in the war, holding a defensive line in the Far East, and then "slugging with air at West Europe, to be followed by a land attack as soon as possible."

The British preferred to first wear down the Germans with blows against North Africa and other points along their periphery. But Eisenhower and his staff drew up a plan called Roundup for a cross-Channel attack within a year, which Marshall and Roosevelt endorsed. In May, during ten days in Britain, Eisenhower found that the Chief of the Imperial General Staff, General Alan Brooke, and others of the British high command had little confidence in the plan.

During the spring, Marshall had silently assessed his capacity for larger duty. When he described him to Roosevelt, the President felt that Eisenhower had just the kind of personality to master the terrible problems of welding the armed forces of two nations for the first time in history into an efficient and flexible coalition. Eisenhower's short visit to England gave the British equal confidence in him. This redoubled Marshall's intention to name him commander of the European theater. "The chief of staff told me this A.M. that it's *possible I* may go to England in command," Eisenhower wrote after seeing Marshall in June. "It's a big job . . . the biggest American job of the war." A few days later: "The chief of staff says I'm the guy." Most assumed nevertheless that when Roundup was launched in the spring of 1943, Marshall would be the commander, with Eisenhower as Chief of Staff.

After two weeks of briefings, he was off for London and Allied headquarters in Grosvenor Square, soon redesignated "Eisenhowerplatz." He landed in England without speeches or welcoming marches or children laden with flowers, his last such quiet welcome for nineteen years.

With his staff, Eisenhower insisted on a "happy family" and constantly reminded them, "I want to see a big crowd of friends around here." He was a magnet for loyalty. "I love that man," said his Chief of Staff, General Walter Bedell "Beetle" Smith. "The sun rises and sets on him for me." The British Admiral Andrew Cunningham later said that "it was not long before one recognized him as the really great man he is—forceful, able, direct and far-seeing, with great charm of manner and always with a rather naive wonder at attaining the high position in which he found himself."

With war reporters around his office, he was modest, cheerful, relaxed, unusually candid, calling them "quasi-members of my staff." To the GIs, Eisenhower was no distant figure like MacArthur but a

paternal presence, griping about the "Big Brass" as if he were not one of them. He told Carl Sandburg, "When they called me Uncle Ike or . . . just plain Ike, I knew everything was going well."

Readers in the United States soon learned of the General's homely tastes and habits—how he had turned down a lavish Claridge's suite in favor of simpler quarters at the Dorchester, his talk about "my hometown Abilene," his passion for golf and Wild West novels. In Abilene, reporters asked the eighty-year-old Ida about her son's first steps to greatness. People in theaters across America watched Eisenhower's face grow dark as he spoke of the Nazis and then, as he spoke of the force being amassed to crush them, flashing the contagious smile said to be worth twenty divisions.

Anglo-American relations were aggravated by shortages of men and materiel, strategy differences, resentments, and jealousies as Americans supplanted Englishmen as the senior partners in the European theater. Eisenhower was to fuse the two factions into a smoothly operating coalition. He told his new colleagues that solidarity between Americans and Englishmen was his "religion." His talents in getting along with men of inimical backgrounds and making them like each other, gained during long years in the Army, were fully mobilized. When a British general told him that a drunken American officer had boasted that the Yanks would show the British how to fight, Eisenhower said, "I'll make the son of a bitch swim back to America."

November 1942: In a dank room deep in the Rock of Gibraltar, Eisenhower poses with two aides, Lieutenant Commander Harry Butcher and Major Ernest "Tex" Lee, just before launching Operation Torch.

Τhe invasion of North Africa.
*Above:* Troops landing light guns near Oran and tank-destroyer men finding cover on a hill overlooking El Guettar Valley, Tunisia.
*Opposite:* Americans filing ashore from small landing craft near Oran.

By autumn 1942, the Allies agreed to postpone Roundup and forgo Sledgehammer, a risky plan to open a Second Front late in the year in order to divert German pressure from the Russians. They decided instead to strike against Axis forces in French North Africa. In his September diary, Eisenhower noted that the operation, code-named Torch, was "something of a quite desperate nature and which depends only in minor degree upon the professional preparations we can make or upon the wisdom of our own military decisions. In a way it is like the return of Napoleon from Elba—if the guess as to psychological reaction is correct, we may gain a tremendous advantage in this war; if the guess is wrong, it would be almost certain that we will gain nothing and will lose a lot." The opponent was to be a disoriented, under-equipped Vichy French Army, but after eleven months at war, the largest force the United States could gather against it was two divisions.

On invasion eve at the start of November 1942, Eisenhower and his staff climbed into Flying Fortresses and flew to their headquarters in a dripping cave deep inside the Rock of Gibraltar. In his diary he wrote, "The symbol of the solidity of the British Empire, the hallmark of safety and security at home, the jealously guarded rock that has played a tremendous part in the trade development of the English race! An American is in charge, and I am he. . . . I simply must have a grandchild or I'll never have the fun of telling this when I'm fishing, gray-bearded, on the banks of a quiet bayou in the deep South."

Eisenhower had been brought into a war zone for the first time in his life. His biographer Stephen Ambrose has written that in his first great command, the General was "unsure of himself, hesitant, often depressed, irritable, liable to make snap judgments on insufficient information, defensive in both his mood and his tactics." It did not help that the early stages of his task were as much political as military. Allied planners were preoccupied by the need to blunt resistance from the French commanders and civil authorities in power in North Africa: Most were aligned with the Vichy regime of Marshal Henri Pétain and hated the Free French General Charles de Gaulle, who in London was kept unapprised of the assault. President Roosevelt's roving political adviser, Robert Murphy, had searched for leaders who might rally the local population to the Allied cause and secure the French fleet. He focused on General Henri Giraud, who was briefly commander of the French Ninth Army before his imprisonment in May 1940 and his escape in April 1942.

Allied soldiers landed at Casablanca, Algiers, Oran. On all fronts, Frenchmen resisted, Allied troops died. Now, Admiral Jean Darlan, commander in chief of the Vichy armed forces and a collaborator with Hitler, was the key. Eisenhower later wrote that "in the long run, we could defeat the local French forces." But "that would also defeat our hope of making the French in Africa our allies—and would hamper later operations in the base from which we would be attacking the Axis. . . . On the other hand, if I should decide to deal with Darlan,

we were assured of an immediate ceasefire, no more casualties, and a chance at Tunisia." With the support of his American and British superiors, Eisenhower acceded to the bargain soon known as the Darlan Deal: In exchange for making the Admiral Governor-General of French North Africa, the Allies would tolerate Vichy officials and Vichy laws, including anti-Semitic decrees.

American and British critics asked if Eisenhower and the United States were allying themselves with a man like Darlan, why was this war being fought? The General wrote his son, "I have been called a Fascist and almost a Hitlerite." He told a colleague, "I can't understand why these long-haired, starry-eyed guys keep gunning for me. I'm no reactionary. Christ on the mountain! I'm as idealistic as hell." Eisenhower's surprise at the public reaction betrayed the limits of his training in the moral and political dimensions of warfare. Churchill cabled him, "Anything for the battle, but the politics will have to be sorted out later on."

Eisenhower was a logical whipping boy because the North African campaign was flagging. Darlan's involvement helped to keep the French from fighting Americans but did not fire them up for doing battle with Germans. By December 1942, Allied troops were mired in Tunisian fields transformed by rains into a vast quagmire. On Christmas Eve, as Eisenhower took dinner in a Tunis farmhouse, Darlan was mysteriously assassinated. That same week Marshall ordered Eisenhower to "delegate your international diplomatic problems to your subordinates and give your complete attention to the battle in Tunisia."

At his Algiers headquarters, suffering from influenza, Eisenhower heard rumors that when his forces linked up with the westward-moving British Army, he would lose his job to General Harold Alexander, the Supreme British Commander in the desert. Churchill was displeased with Eisenhower's opposition to an early attack on Tunis. Roosevelt was said to regard the General's retention as "politically inexpedient"—especially after Eisenhower earned renewed public scorn in January 1943 by appointing Marcel Peyrouton, a notorious fascist, as Governor of Algeria. In late January, when Churchill and Roosevelt met at Casablanca, the President noted that "Ike seems jittery."

Nevertheless both leaders knew that they bore equal responsibility for Darlan. They were impressed by Eisenhower's ability to run a mixed staff, and although the British had more troop strength, Churchill knew that the French could not be made to serve smoothly under a British commander. Eisenhower kept command of the Torch forces and was given command of the British Eighth Army as soon as it reached Tunisia. To strengthen his authority, Marshall recommended his promotion to full general. Eisenhower's aide Harry Butcher noted that Marshall's "whole attitude toward Ike was almost that of father to son."

In North Africa, the Allies took over command of the air and rushed firepower to the front lines, foiling Germany's efforts to break

Spring 1943: Eisenhower, accompanied by Lieutenant General George Patton, inspects the Tunisian battlefront.

Allied supply lines and defend its own. In mid-February, at the Faid Pass, Field Marshal Erwin Rommel's Afrika Corps destroyed an American tank battalion, overran a battalion of artillery, and isolated those American troops that were left. Another defeat followed two days later at the Kasserine Pass. Only American firepower and German deficiencies forestalled an Allied humiliation. Eisenhower wrote Marshall that the men "are now mad and ready to fight." When the British Eighth Army and its commander, Bernard Law Montgomery, reached the Tunisian frontier, the Allies had the Germans surrounded.

Alexander and the British insisted on a plan for the final assault that would exclude the Americans. Eisenhower warned that if the American people felt that their troops would not have a prominent role in the European theater, they would be more likely to insist on a strategy of Asia First. He went on to note that since Americans would do the bulk of the fighting in the final conquest of Germany, they had better gain confidence now in their ability to fight the Germans. The British relented. By early May, the British First and Eighth Armies had combined with the American II Corps to clear the Axis from Tunisia. German and Italian forces in North Africa signed an unconditional surrender. Allied forces captured 275,000 Axis troops. Eisenhower wrote Mamie, "I only wish that it were the *final* battle of this war and that I could be catching the next plane for home and *you!!* But I'm afraid that happy day is still a long way off."

Flying over the Mediterranean, he looked down on an Allied convoy sailing toward Egypt, symbol of the triumph. The British adviser for North Africa, Harold Macmillan, touched his arm: "There, General, are the fruits of your victory." Smiling, with tears in his eyes, Eisenhower said, "Ours, you mean. Ours, the victory that we have all won together." From Abilene, Gladys Harding Brooks wrote him, "The fall of Tunisia! With kings and Queens—a Prime Minister, the President of our United States—here and there—all sending you 'Congratulations' as well as hundreds of others all over the world—May we too send ours and just repeat again and again how wonderful we all think you are & oh! how proud we are of you!!!"

Eisenhower's wartime circle was bound by the pressures of battle, shared sense of purpose, and absence of family. His driver and secretary

Touring the North African front, the General watches machine gunners and stops for a meal.

46

Kay Summersby, a slim Irishwoman from County Cork who had once modeled for Worth of Paris, recalled that "our relationships seemed deeper, more meaningful and richer than any we had known before." It was Eisenhower who told her that her American fiancé had been killed in North Africa. Her feelings evolved from adoration to romance. Many years later, dying of cancer and deep in debt, she dictated an unverifiable memoir portraying the General as torn between his desire to marry her, his ambitions, and his commitment to his wife. She claimed that he vainly tried to consummate their relationship and that he spoke of their trying to have a child together.

Mamie Eisenhower, staying in Washington for the war's duration, heard the rumors about her husband's aide. Since Icky's death, she had been afflicted by fears of airplanes and closed places, of threats to the safety of her remaining son and husband. She avoided movie theaters for fear that seeing the General's image in a newsreel would open the floodgates of her anxieties. She read mystery thrillers through the night and lost thirty pounds. After reading one of her anxious letters, her husband replied, "Stop worrying about me. The few women I've met are nothing—absolutely nothing compared to you, and besides, I've neither the time nor the youth to worry about them."

July 1943 brought the invasion of Sicily with 3,300 ships and a half million men, the largest amphibious invasion in history. Directing the effort from Malta, Eisenhower hoped that it would start the process

At an Algiers press conference, June 1943, Eisenhower and Marshall, for whom he had "unlimited admiration."

June 1943, Algiers: Eisenhower appreciates the performance as Winston Churchill displays his trademark V-for-Victory greeting. After North Africa, Eisenhower wished to invade Sicily, Sardinia, and Corsica, and then western Italy. The British Prime Minister has flown to Algiers to persuade Eisenhower to go for the Italian boot, noting that capture of Rome "would be a very great achievement." Eisenhower later wrote that during such private debates on strategy, Churchill "used humor and pathos with equal facility, and drew on everything from the Greek classics to Donald Duck."

July 1943: The invasion of
Sicily, using 3,300 ships, the
largest amphibious operation
in history.

*Opposite (top to bottom and
right):* A British Eighth Army
squad seeking Axis resistance
in Catania.

The capture of Melilli.
Searching for snipers after
the conquest of Messina.

Civilians being treated by
American medical corpsmen
in St. Stefano.

August 1943 *(opposite):* After Sicily's liberation, Eisenhower and his uneasy British comrade-in-arms, Bernard Law Montgomery, take coffee at Messina.

The invasion of Italy begins: The Allies establish a beachhead at Salerno as a landing craft takes a direct hit.

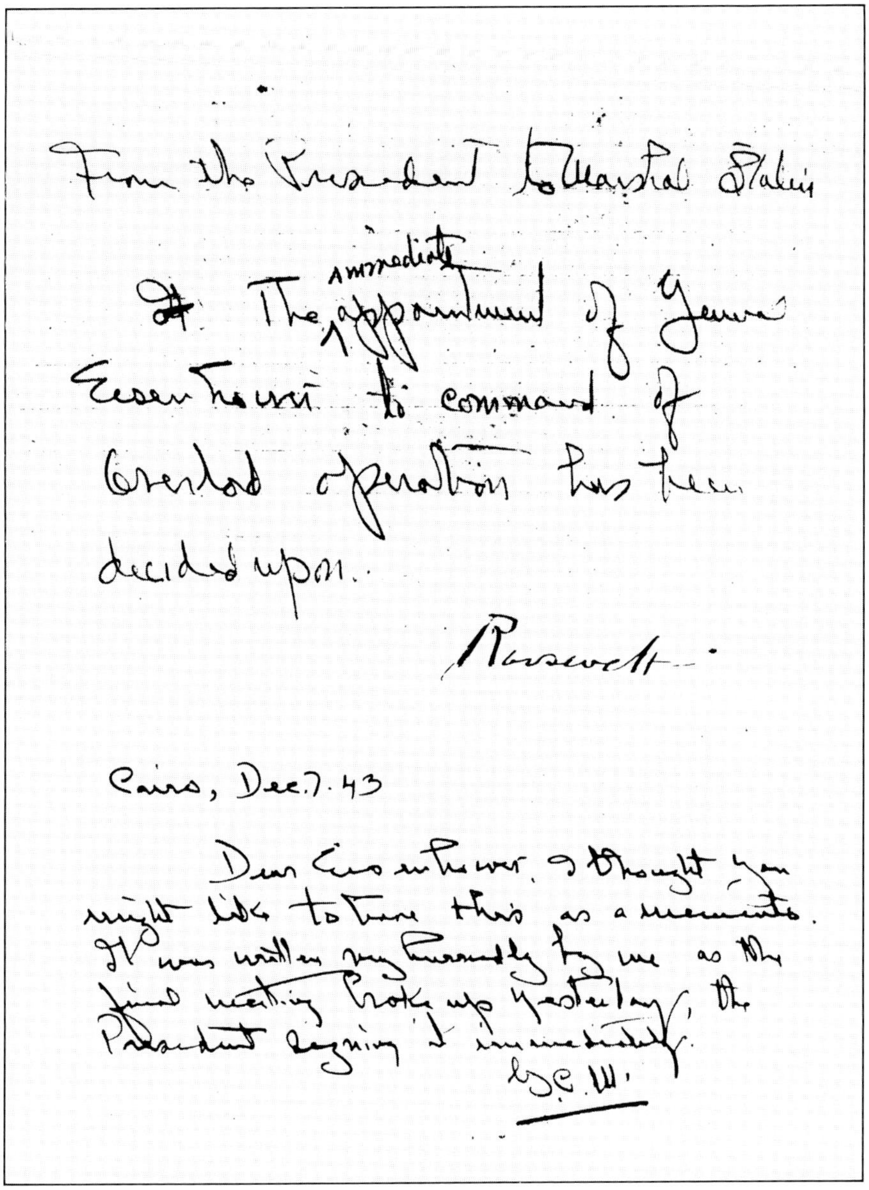

From the President to Marshal Stalin

The immediate appointment of General Eisenhower to command of Overlord operation has been decided upon.

Roosevelt

Cairo, Dec. 7. 43

Dear Eisenhower, I thought you might like to have this as a memento. It was written very hurriedly by me as the final meeting broke up yesterday, the President signing it immediately.

G.C.M.

Eisenhower and President Franklin Roosevelt at Casablanca, January 1943, and Tunis, November 1943.

The note to Stalin recording Eisenhower's appointment as commander of the invasion of France. At bottom is Marshall's graceful message to Eisenhower about an appointment that, as Roosevelt had said, should by rights have gone to Marshall.

leading to the surrender of Benito Mussolini's Fascist Italy and liberation of the Mediterranean, as well as tie down large numbers of German troops, which would ease pressure on the Russians. But two German divisions held off half a million Allied troops for thirty-eight days and inflicted twenty thousand casualties before the island was conquered.

Eisenhower moved to exploit the great buildup of men and materiel in North Africa and Sicily to drive Italy out of the war. After a first Allied bombing raid against Rome in mid-July, Mussolini was dismissed and arrested. The Germans began rushing troops into northern Italy and planned an occupation south of Rome. Eisenhower wished to propose an honorable peace to Italians on radio, with the Allies coming to Italy as liberators to "rid you of the Germans and . . . the horrors of war." After a month of Anglo-American negotiation, Eisenhower was told he could offer the Italians a role against the Nazis, but only after they publicly surrendered: They should announce an armistice, send their fleet and air force to Allied territory, and join against the Germans. But by mid-August, the Germans had moved nineteen di-

A nzio: As the invasion forces secured the Salerno beachhead and approached Naples at the end of September, Eisenhower had escalated the stakes by demanding the capture of Rome, but not through the formidable mountains. He ordered an amphibious end run around enemy lines to break German defenses south of Rome. Thus, in January, the landing by two divisions at Anzio, the start of four months of fighting.

Eisenhower oversees the invasion of Italy.

*Top:* Listening to a report, along with Lieutenant General Mark Clark *(in helmet)* and Vice Admiral H. K. Hewitt *(right)*.

*Middle:* With Butcher and Montgomery.

*Bottom:* Admiring a dog honored for wounds received while attacking a German machine-gun nest.

*Overleaf:* Eisenhower and Clark *(right)* cross a pontoon bridge over the Volturno River, north of Naples.

5 M.P.H.
80 FEET
DISPERSAL

visions into Italy. The Italians knew that if they surrendered before the Americans reached Rome, the Germans would simply overthrow the government.

On September 3, the Eighth Army crossed the Strait of Messina and landed on the Italian toe. General Giuseppe Costellano of the Italian General Staff, representing the new Italian leader, Marshal Pietro Badoglio, signed the armistice. Then, frightened that the Allied forces driving toward Rome could not hold off the Germans, Badoglio demanded cancelation of the armistice and the imminent Allied landings. Furious, Eisenhower "played a little poker." He privately threatened Badoglio with the "most serious consequences," and as scheduled announced on Rome radio that "the Italian government has surrendered its armed forces unconditionally." Granting an armistice "this instant," he urged Italians to "help eject the German aggressor from Italian soil."

Eisenhower's gamble succeeded: An hour later, Badoglio broadcast his agreed-upon proclamation ordering Italian armed forces to fight the Germans. Nevertheless the Germans took Rome. Badoglio and other key Italian leaders fled for the south and Allied protection. The Italian Army disbanded. Italy swiftly became an occupied country. The Allies won the Italian fleet but little more. Through October and November, there was stalemate, with the Germans established behind a "Winter Line" of defensive positions across the Italian peninsula considerably south of Rome. In January, two divisions landed at Anzio, launching a costly four-month operation. On June 4, the last German troops left Rome. By then Eisenhower's and the world's attention had shifted to the attack across the English Channel.

Eisenhower and most of his colleagues had long supposed that Marshall would command the invasion of France, Operation Overlord. Touring Tunisian battlefields in November 1943, Roosevelt told Eisenhower, "I hate to think that fifty years from now, practically nobody will know who George Marshall was. That is one of the reasons why I want George to have the big command—he is entitled to establish his place in history as a great general." Eisenhower gloomily contemplated returning to Washington to replace Marshall as Chief of Staff. As his son John later wrote in his history of the Anglo-American war alliance, it had "never seriously occurred" to Eisenhower that he might be given Overlord.

Roosevelt wanted three commands rolled into one for Marshall—Overlord, the Mediterranean theater, and the invasion of southern France. The British refused. The President was reluctant to offer the General a post that might seem a step down. Choosing Eisenhower had its own logic. By now Eisenhower had commanded three amphibious invasions; he had been given a day-to-day education in preserving a joint command and bridging differences over strategy and tactics; he was wildly popular. In December 1943, stopping in Tunisia after his meetings with Stalin and Churchill in Tehran, Roosevelt told him, "Well, Ike, you are going to command Overlord."

60

The capture of Rome. An American takes a bead on German snipers. Britons and Americans congratulate one another. On June 4, 1944, the last German troops left the ancient capital. Two days later, the world's attention was riveted on the north coast of France.

That fall, Senator Arthur Capper of Kansas had written Eisenhower asking him to become next year's Republican candidate for President. The General had by military custom never voted and had never revealed his party preference. He replied that he had "a gigantic job" to do, "and for any soldier to turn his attention elsewhere would constitute a neglect of duty to his country."

After a New Year's visit to Mamie in Washington and White Sulphur Springs ("Don't come back again till it's over, Ike—I can't stand losing you again"), the Supreme Commander returned to London. Distracted by the city, he reestablished headquarters outside London and installed himself in a small house called Telegraph Cottage, where he lived while overseeing planning for the assault against Fortress Europe. To overcome German advantages in manpower and land com-

March 1944: Eisenhower and Montgomery at a tank demonstration outside London as they plan Operation Overlord, the invasion of Fortress Europe. At left is Arthur Tedder, the Supreme Commander's British deputy.

munication, the Allies had to depend on surprise, control of the air and sea, and their ability to choose a narrow front for intensive bombardment. Only Eisenhower could see the problem whole. The strain began to tell. "Ike looks worn and tired," wrote Harry Butcher in May. "He looks older now than at any time since I have been with him." He spent much of the spring seeing the troops who would have to carry rifles onto Normandy Beach under German fire, for success or failure would ultimately hinge on them.

Overlord depended also on the weather. If there were storms, landing craft could be overturned in the water. Troops could be seasick when they hit the beaches. Air superiority could be threatened. On Saturday evening, June 3, 1944, two days before D-Day, Eisenhower's chief weatherman, Royal Air Force Group Captain J. M. Stagg, warned that skies would be stormy and overcast. If the great crusade lacked air superiority, the landings would be too risky. The General postponed the operation for twenty-four hours. The next evening, it was raining outside. Stagg told Eisenhower and his staff that bombers and fighters ought to be able to operate on Monday night, although hampered by clouds. Others were more dubious. All knew that another delay would mean postponement to June 19, the next day by which tidal conditions would be right again.

Eisenhower said, "The question is just how long can you hang this operation on the end of a limb and let it hang there." Beetle Smith noted the "loneliness and isolation of a commander at a time when such a momentous decision was to be taken by him, with full knowledge that failure or success rests on his individual decision." Looking out at the night rain, Eisenhower gave the order. The next morning, before dawn, he awoke as violent wind and rain shook his command trailer. It was not too late to postpone the operation. He dressed, drank coffee, consulted his circle. Then he paused to think and said, "O.K., we'll go." The commanders ran to their posts.

As the mighty surge onto the Continent began, he paced a cinder path outside his trailer and rubbed some lucky coins he had kept from the victories in North Africa and Italy. In his wallet, he carried two messages—the first congratulating his troops if they established them-

April 1944 (opposite): In formal clothes, Churchill is photographed at a rifle range, flanked by Eisenhower and General Omar Bradley. Eisenhower told the Prime Minister, "I assure you that the coming winter will see the Allied forces on the borders of Germany itself."

June 1944: Eisenhower bids farewell to paratroopers about to take off for the first assault on France. A private cried, "Look out, Hitler, here we come!" Another soldier promised the General a postwar job on his Texas ranch.

Eisenhower had been warned that 70 percent of this unit might die in the invasion. After the last plane roared into the skies, he sagged into his car, his eyes filling with tears.

D-Day: June 6, 1944.
   *Opposite:* Ships fill the channel while balloons protect them from enemy strafers.
   *Top:* Troops poised for invasion.
   *Middle:* Reinforcements arriving after the initial landings.
   *Bottom:* Onto the beaches.

selves at Normandy, the second accepting personal blame after defeat. The news from the French coast made him by turns elated and anxious. On the British and Canadian beaches, opposition was reported light; on Utah, Americans were well established; on Omaha, troops were staggering under surprisingly heavy German fire. With only 2,500 casualties, more than 175,000 Allied soldiers entered Fortress Europe. On the morning of Wednesday, June 7, Eisenhower rode the British minelayer *Apollo* to the beachhead, where all around he could see nothing but Allied ships and planes.

On June 19, the worst storm in twenty years struck the beaches of Normandy. The Supreme Commander scribbled, "Thank the gods of war we went when we did!" By the Fourth of July, he reported to Washington that the one millionth Allied soldier had landed in France. Revisiting the beach at Normandy twenty years later, he said, "My mind goes back to the fact that my son was graduated from West Point on D-Day, and on the very day he was graduating, men . . . stormed these beaches, not to gain anything for themselves, not to fulfill any ambitions that America had for conquest but just to preserve freedom, to establish systems of self-government in the world. . . . They had families who grieved for them. But they never had the great experience of going through life like my son."

In France, American tanks were stalled by the hedgerow country. Montgomery had failed in his promise to take Caen. These frustrations exacerbated his differences with Eisenhower. Eisenhower wished to exploit American manpower and material resources with constant attack. Montgomery preferred "unbalancing the enemy while keeping well-balanced myself." Eisenhower prodded Churchill to "persuade Monty to get on his bicycle and start moving." In mid-July, the Field Marshal unleashed another offensive, code-named Goodwood, using "the heaviest and most concentrated air attack in support of ground troops ever attempted," which took Caen but little else. An angry Eisenhower noted that it had taken more than seven thousand tons of bombs to gain seven miles.

Eisenhower's West Point classmate, General Omar Bradley, conceived a successful breakout plan, code-named Cobra, which was activated at the end of July. On August 1, General George Patton's Third Army began racing through Brittany. With the German left flank open, Eisenhower ordered the "great bulk" of Patton's forces to "the task of completing the destruction of the German Army." By mid-August, after Canadian forces took Falaise and linked up with Patton in Argentan, two German armies were encircled.

Almost jubilant, Eisenhower nonetheless warned reporters that Hitler and his troops would "fight to the bitter end." On August 27, when the Supreme Commander arrived with Omar Bradley in the French capital, Parisians mobbed and kissed them. Eisenhower agreed to a Montgomery plan, code-named Market-Garden, using the Airborne Army and British Second Army to throw a bridgehead across the lower Rhine at Arnhem. It failed. Devoting resources to Arnhem

# BACK 'EM UP

# BUY *EXTRA* BONDS

forced the Allies to forfeit reopening and using the critical port of Antwerp for supply movements soon enough for any prospect of victory in 1944.

"People of the strength and warlike tendencies of the Germans do not give in," Eisenhower said that fall. "They must be beaten to the ground." With Allied resources superior to those of the Germans, he waged a war of attrition through rain, mud, and fog. In December 1944, the desperate Hitler gambled with a surprise attack in the Ardennes region of Belgium and Luxembourg, the start of the Battle of the Bulge, the largest battle in which the U.S. Army has ever been engaged.

Montgomery wished to take the first blow and then counterattack after the Germans had been stopped. Believing that the attacking German divisions were battered and understrength, Eisenhower preferred to hit back with power and speed. He thought he had won Montgomery's agreement to a counterattack on New Year's Day, 1945. Told that it would not be staged until at least two days later, he took command as never before and confronted the Field Marshal. The counterattack began on January 3 and took a month to drive the Germans back to their original line. When the battle was over, German armor was mostly gone. After breaking through Hitler's West Wall, Eisenhower's forces could rip through Germany with little resistance. But the cost was eighty-one thousand Allied casualties—seventy-seven thousand of these American, the heaviest battle toll in American history.

Allied air forces late that winter were running as many as eleven thousand sorties per day. Before D-Day, when the British complained about civilian casualties, Eisenhower had threatened to resign unless bombers were deployed against the French railroad system instead of, as General Carl "Tooey" Spaatz demanded, against German aircraft factories and oil refineries. He later called his insistence on what was called the Transportation Plan his single greatest contribution to the success of Overlord, isolating Normandy so that the Germans could not use their manpower and logistical advantages to overwhelm the

Allied invaders. By late 1944, Spaatz's oil campaign was preventing German control of the air and was on the verge of eliminating German fuel reserves.

Early in the spring of 1945, Eisenhower made what some critics later considered his great mistake of the war by refusing British demands to race the Russians to Berlin. By March the Allied Expeditionary Force was more than two hundred miles from the German capital, the Red Army only thirty-five. Omar Bradley suggested that taking Berlin would require about one hundred thousand casualties—"a pretty stiff price to pay for a prestige objective," since Berlin was deep within the occupation zone ceded to the Soviet Union by Roosevelt, Churchill, and Stalin at Yalta.

Eisenhower genuinely hoped to build a postwar alliance in which Russia and the West would act in concert. Patton was ready to turn against the Russians, Montgomery to arrange the weapons of surrendering Germans to swiftly rearm the Wehrmacht if needed for early war with the Soviet Union. Eisenhower argued that racing the Soviets

August 1944: In a scene out of *A Midsummer Night's Dream,* troops move through a forest in southern France. That same month, the victory march down the Champs-Elysées in Paris.

Eisenhower inspects the European battlefront *(opposite and overleaves).*
The General lunches with General Omar Bradley and Major General Ira Wyche in Maunville, France.

Spring 1945: Eisenhower enters Germany in triumph.

*Opposite:* With Lieutenant General William Simpson and General Raymond McLain at Jülich.

*Overleaf, left top:* Eisenhower and Bradley on the Rhine's eastern bank for the first time.

*Overleaf, left bottom:* At Oipe.

*Overleaf, right:* At Jülich.

In December 1944, the desperate Hitler gambles with a surprise attack in the Ardennes region of Belgium and Luxembourg, the start of the Battle of the Bulge, causing eighty-one thousand Allied casualties. Seventy-seven thousand of these are American, the heaviest battle toll in American history. Only by January 21, 1945, are the Germans driven back to their original line. Here, American infantrymen crawl under barbed wire between U.S. and German forces.

April 12, 1945: On the day of Roosevelt's death in Warm Springs, Georgia, Eisenhower is shown a German concentration camp near Gotha. He wrote, "I have never at any other time experienced an equal sense of shock. I visited every nook and cranny of the camp because I felt it my duty to be in a position from then on to testify at first hand about these things in case there ever grew up at home the belief or assumption that 'the stories of Nazi brutality were just propaganda.' " Standing under a gallows, he listens to liberated inmates describe atrocities. Nazi methods of torture are demonstrated. Shown the remains of other prisoners, Eisenhower orders a photographer to record the scene so that future generations may never doubt what happened here.

for Berlin would poison postwar collaboration before it began. His grandson David later wrote in his history of the General at war that "perhaps he was realistic enough to suspect that genuine peacetime Allied-Soviet cooperation would not be possible" but was "stirred by the possibility, which he saw as an extension of a successful war policy," and "opposed the all-too-quick demonization of the Russians."

Eisenhower's reluctance to demonize the Russians was influenced by his outrage at the Germans. He toured a concentration camp, saw naked corpses piled to the ceiling, talked to inmates. He wrote Mamie, "I never dreamed that such cruelty, bestiality and savagery could really exist in this world!" He wrote Marshall, "The things I saw beggar description. . . . I made the visit deliberately in order to be in a position to give *first-hand* evidence of these things if ever, in the future, there develops a tendency to charge these allegations merely to 'propaganda.' " He insisted that reporters and British and American politicians see the camps and sent photographs of them to Churchill. He reportedly said he was ashamed to have a German surname.

Eisenhower's feeling about the Germans did not lead him to a deliberate, secret strategy of genocide against a million German prisoners after the war, as alleged in a sensational 1989 volume by a Canadian author. Coping with severe European food shortages and while "urgently requesting" more shipments, Eisenhower not irrationally gave fifth priority to German prisoners, after Allied troops, Allied civilians, displaced persons and concentration camp inmates, and German civilians. One result of this policy and the brutal conditions in the camps was the staggering loss of possibly fifty to a hundred thousand German prisoners, but these Germans did not die because the Supreme Commander wanted retribution.

Early on May 7, 1945, the struggle in Europe was over. A week after Hitler's suicide, the German Chief of Staff, Alfred Jodl, arrived at Eisenhower's French headquarters in Reims. In another room, the Supreme Commander paced and smoked as the German delivered his nation into Allied hands. Then Beetle Smith brought Jodl to Eisenhower, who warned him that he would be held personally accountable if the terms of the unconditional surrender were violated. Exhausted, the central military figure in the victory now dictated a message: "The mission of this Allied force was fulfilled at 0241 local time, May 7, 1945." He slouched and called for a bottle of champagne.

In London, Churchill declared it time for the "greatest outburst of joy in the history of mankind."

Victory in Europe, May 7, 1945: After the signing of the unconditional surrender at Reims, France. Eisenhower's Chief of Staff, General Walter Bedell Smith, and his aide Kay Summersby stand at his left.

# 3.
# "A KIND OF DREAM BOY"

The Supreme Commander was decorated by George VI at Buckingham Palace, kissed on both cheeks by de Gaulle in Paris, and hailed elsewhere as "the greatest strategist since Napoleon." Flown home in President Harry Truman's airplane, he was paraded through shrieking crowds in Washington, New York, West Point, Kansas City, Abilene. Told in July that an atomic bomb existed, Eisenhower advised Truman not to use it because Japan was "already defeated" and the United States "should avoid shocking world opinion."

As viceroys over Germany, Eisenhower and Marshal Georgi Zhukov passed many hours after VE-Day comparing American and Soviet political philosophies and thinking aloud about their families and hopes. At a banquet, Eisenhower declared that what he and Zhukov wanted was peace, even "if we have to fight for it." In August, Zhukov flew with him to Moscow, where Stalin gave Eisenhower the honor of standing atop the Lenin Tomb to review a victory parade. That week, Americans dropped the Bomb on Hiroshima and Nagasaki. The General told reporters that he had been "sure we could keep the peace with Russia. Now I don't know. . . . People are frightened and disturbed all over. Everyone feels insecure again."

During battle he had written Mamie, "When this hectic war is over, I often wonder whether anyone who has carried heavy responsi-

June 1945: After three painful wartime years, Mamie Eisenhower welcomes her husband at National Airport, Washington, D.C.

June 1945: At the Guildhall in London, Eisenhower declares, "I come from the very heart of America. . . . The town where I was born and the one where I was reared are far separated from this great city. Abilene, Kansas, and Denison, Texas, would together equal in size possibly one five-hundredth of a part of great London. . . . But . . . neither London nor Abilene, sisters under the skin, will sell her birthright for physical safety, her liberty for mere existence." At the Arc de Triomphe, Paris, he is decorated by General Charles de Gaulle.

bilities and has had to jump constantly from hither to thither to yon can really settle down. . . . I know that when I find myself contemplating a post-war existence I always pick a little place far from cities (but with someone near enough for occasional bridge) and the two of us just getting brown in the sun (and probably thick in the middle). A dozen cats and dogs, with a horse or two, maybe a place to fish (not too strenuously) and a field in which to shoot a few birds once in a while—I think that's roughly my idea of a good life." Now, back in Washington, his wife found him "changed terrifically," surrounded by staff and confined to rigid schedule: "He belonged to the world and not to me anymore."

He accepted Truman's request to replace Marshall as Chief of Staff and perform what Eisenhower later called the "dreary business" of paring the wartime Army: "The taste of it I had during World War One at a far lower level did nothing to whet my appetite for the task now to be performed at the top." His December 1945 diary: "This job (chief of staff) is as bad as I always thought it would be. . . . I'm astounded and appalled at the size and scope of plans the staff sees as necessary to maintain our security position now and in the future. The cost is terrific. . . . Of course the number-one problem is demobilization, and due to a bundle of misunderstandings I'll soon have to go before Congress personally and give them the facts of life."

There was more and more speculation that the hero of the European theater would run for President of the United States. The drumbeat had begun even before he was back on American soil. As the General recalled, he had "laughed off" the idea until, while riding through the conquered streets of Berlin, Truman promised to ensure that Eisenhower obtained whatever he wanted: "That definitely and specifically includes the Presidency in 1948." By Eisenhower's account, he replied, "I don't know who will be your opponent for the Presidency, but it will not be I." Nonetheless Truman's offer struck him in his "emotional vitals."

After the November 1946 midterm elections, Eisenhower wrote in his diary, "A number of well-meaning friends have suggested a politi-

June 1945 *(opposite):* The victorious General is greeted by President Truman and carried by Jeep up Capitol Hill, where he speaks to Congress. In New York City, he jokes with Mayor Fiorello LaGuardia and is welcomed with ticker tape and confetti.

Returned to Abilene, Eisenhower salutes a homecoming parade and, at photographers' request, poses with his mother on the porch of the family homestead. During the war, he was told that she had grown senile and might not recognize him. Ida died in 1946, after which the house was opened to the public.

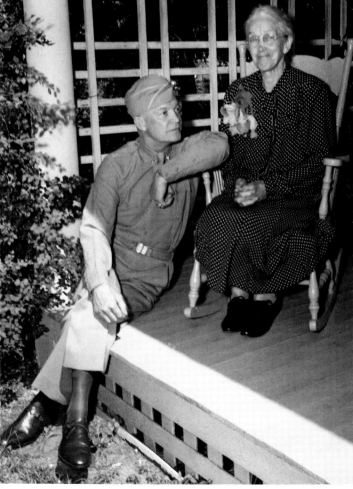

6 December 1945

Dear Marshal Zhukov:

You may be aware of the fact that I was prevented, because of sickness, from returning to Europe late last month. One of the things I was particularly anxious to do was to see you, for several reasons.

Firstly, I wanted to assure you of my very deep appreciation for your friendly and cooperative attitude toward me during the months since the German surrender. It was an association that was most valuable and satisfactory from my viewpoint and I truly hope you feel the same. I hope you will always permit me to call you "friend".

Secondly, I wanted to say goodbye to the principal members of your staff, particularly those with whom I have frequently come in contact, and had hoped personally to introduce my successor to you and to them.

Finally, I wanted to tell you again of my hope that you would find it possible to visit our Country next Spring.

I truly feel that if the same type of association that you and I have experienced over the past several months could be established and maintained between large numbers of Soviet and American personnel, both military and civil, we would do much in promoting mutual understanding, confidence and faith between our two peoples. I know that during the entire period my own admiration, respect and affection for the Red Army and its great leaders, and for the Russian people all the way up to the Generalissimo himself, constantly increased.

I should like to request that at any time you feel that I might do anything for you personally or that I might be helpful in promoting the friendships that I feel are so valuable to the world, I will be more than glad to respond to your suggestions, so far as it is in my power to do so.

Again goodbye and good luck.

Very sincerely,

/s/ DDE (Sgd) DWIGHT D. EISENHOWER

Marshal of the Soviet Union
Georgi Konstantinovich Zhukov
Commander-in-Chief,
Soviet Forces in Germany
Berlin.

General Eisenhower and Marshal Zhukov dine in Berlin (opposite). In Moscow, Eisenhower visits the Tretyakov Gallery and joins Stalin and Ambassador Averell Harriman atop the Lenin Tomb for a victory celebration. As the Cold War gained force, the possibility of a Zhukov trip to the United States, as mentioned in Eisenhower's December 1945 letter, evaporated. Eisenhower never saw his Russian friend again, except as President in 1955, when Soviet leaders brought the Marshal to the Geneva summit, perhaps to evoke information that Eisenhower would not confide to others he had not known so intimately.

cal career for me. They seem to listen to my 'no' with their tongues in their cheeks. I have been on an intensive strain since 1938, when I had my last leave save for five days this past summer. I'm suspicious of anyone who believes he could take over the presidency successfully in these days and times. International reactions are bad enough, but they are insignificant compared to domestic issues. I know nothing of the long, tedious process whereby certain labor leaders have become dictators. Yet all my sympathies are with the workers (my youth was one of such hard work, and my memories of my father's life so clear that I could do nothing else). . . . [A]lthough everyone believes in cooperation (the single key) as a principle, no one is ready to abandon immediate advantage or position in practicing cooperation. Moral regeneration, revival of patriotism, clear realization that progress in any great segment is not possible without progress for the whole, all these are necessary."

After Eisenhower's appointment as Supreme Allied Commander, his West Point roommate John Henry Dykes had written him, "This

E isenhower and his wife and son call on the British royal family in 1946.

A postwar painting showing Eisenhower's (and MacArthur's) new place among other great figures in the history of the United States Army.

will lead to the Presidency in ten or fifteen years." He replied, "I don't think so, but I appreciate your kindness." Now he loomed above the American political horizon. Few knew what he privately believed; fewer still knew his party affiliation. This did not deter such varied leaders as Eleanor Roosevelt and Truman, Governor Thomas Dewey of New York and Congressman Richard Nixon of California from suggesting him for President in the years after VE-Day. The columnist Walter Lippmann wrote a friend that the Eisenhower legend was "justified on his human qualities, but it takes no account of his intellectual equipment and his real experience. He is not a real figure in our public life, but a kind of dream boy embodying all the unsatisfied wishes of all the people who are discontented with things as they are."

As Chief of Staff, Eisenhower was enmeshed in routine far beneath the august excitement of the wartime command. For years he had dealt with prime ministers, presidents, and kings, and had not been awed. Sometimes he reminisced about Roosevelt—the difficulty of pinning him down, his condescension, the practical jokes he played on the people who worked for him. Eisenhower said that "Roosevelt was essentially a cruel man." He asserted that as a younger officer, he had once had to carry the President off to bed after too many cocktails: "I like a highball or two myself, but I'll tell you one thing. Nobody's ever going to have to put *me* to bed." As for the incumbent President, Eisenhower and Truman were outwardly cordial. In the circularity of American history, one of his brothers had shared a Kansas City rooming house with Truman. But Eisenhower privately thought him overpartisan: "A fine man who, in the middle of a stormy lake, knows nothing of swimming."

He had always been mistrustful and was often repelled by politics and partisans. The elected official was no citizen of stature in Abilene. Exposure to congressional maneuvering while an Army man—promotions requested for powerful constituents, meddling in war strategy, posturing at hearings before newsreel cameras—did not increase his admiration. He found the concept of patronage "wicked" and "nauseating." He privately noted that "the voteseeker rarely hesitates to appeal to all that is selfish in mankind." Politics was "a combination of gossip, innuendo, sly character assassination and outright lies" in which "the demagogue tries to develop a saleable list of items to hold before the public."

Like one of his military heroes, Robert E. Lee, he believed that "duty" was the most beautiful word in the English language. World War II had brought him a world following. He wished to ensure that it was used in a great cause and not hijacked by self-seeking politicians. Sadly he watched his old boss MacArthur as he vainly stalked the Republican mandarins, reducing himself as he violated the boundary between military command and partisanship. "I won't drag this uniform through politics," Eisenhower once said, grasping his lapels. "It's been all my life."

What allure the White House held for Eisenohower was less in what programs he could enact than the unifying qualities of decency, self-restraint, and moderation he could advance among Americans. In 1947, he complained to a friend in strictest confidence that the Democrats were a hopeless mixture of "extremes on the right, extremes on the left, with political chicanery and expediency shot through the whole business." His passion was to build a national consensus. He exalted "the fellow who is standing in the middle and battling both extremes." He wrote his brother Milton in October 1947 that he would yield only to "a terrific popular pressure" that forced the politicians to stop their machinations and respond; but "we are not children and we know that under the political party system of this country it would certainly be nothing less than a miracle." Yet he wondered aloud to

93

June 1947: John Eisenhower's marriage to an Army daughter, Barbara Jean Thompson, Fort Myer, Virginia.

Lippmann, "You don't suppose a man could ever be nominated by both parties, do you?"

Polls found that both Democratic and Republican voters preferred Eisenhower as their first choice for President in 1948. Volunteer members of a Draft Eisenhower League pulled money out of envelopes from all regions of the country. In the fall of 1947, Truman's Secretary of the Army, Kenneth Royall, by Royall's account, was sent by the President to remind Eisenhower that if he wanted the next Democratic nomination, he needed only to lift a finger: If the General wished, Truman would run as Vice President. By the end of 1947, Eisenhower had to fish or cut bait. Leonard Finder, a New Hampshire newspaper publisher, notified him that a slate of Eisenhower delegates was being entered in his state's Republican primary, the first in the nation. Unless the General renounced the action, voters across the nation might take his silence as a green light.

Eisenhower privately concluded that the Republicans would draft him only if they felt that a more conventional Republican candidate could not restore their party to the White House. Henry Wallace, Franklin Roosevelt's third-term Vice President, seemed to kill this possibility when he announced that he would run for President as a Progressive. Pundits presumed that this would fracture the Democratic Party. Now there seemed to be no need for Republicans to go to the extreme of nominating Eisenhower to retrieve the White House after sixteen years of exile.

On New Year's Eve, 1948, Eisenhower wrote in his diary that Wallace's move had "completely taken me off the spot. He has increased the confidence of the Republicans that anyone can win for them." He wrote his New Hampshire supporters that he would not "accept nomination to high political office." He presumed that his letter "forever destroyed the possibility for a political career for myself": The probable Republican nominee, Thomas Dewey, would serve until 1957. Then Eisenhower would be sixty-seven, too old to run by the standards of the time.

Writing in later years, Eisenhower used this episode as evidence of his nonchalance about whether he became President or not (and thus his determined self-image as a man who later accepted the job for reasons not of ambition but pure duty). In fact, his withdrawal in 1948 may not have been so voluntary. The circle of New York financiers, board chairmen, and publishers who had been close to Eisenhower since the war—men on whom he would have depended for support— was mainly supporting Dewey. Eisenhower knew that his own candidacy would defy their wish to build an undivided base of support for Dewey. And especially after Wallace's announcement, he knew that if he ran, he might well fail to win the nomination.

Instead, the General wrote a highly successful war memoir, *Crusade in Europe,* for Doubleday, which paid him a flat fee of $635,000, making him well-to-do for the first time in his life. In 1960, he proudly noted in private that the book was "still selling at about three thousand copies a year."

April 1948: Restless as Army Chief of Staff, Eisenhower testifies before the Senate Armed Services Committee, shortly before he gave up smoking.

President of Columbia
University: Eisenhower
watches a football practice
with coach Lou Little.

He accepted the presidency of Columbia University. His July 1947 diary: "In a way it was a 'stampeding' process, except that it had been first mentioned to me more than a year ago. But late this spring a group of the trustees, apparently spearheaded by Mr. Tom Watson [of IBM], began pressuring me to accept, and at the same time another group wanted me to take the head of the Boy Scouts (a most appealing offer), while a group of Midwesterners said they had a senatorship ready to lay in my lap, without a move except a nod from me. Another group was anxious that I consider a commercial venture, but this type of thing was easy to refuse." He hoped he could "do some good, but I don't see why an educator would not have been more suitable in the post. The trustees understand thoroughly two conditions I've laid down. I must convince myself, within a year, that I can be of real service. I must have more recreation time than my average of the past twenty-five years. If either of these conditions is not met, I'll quit." After five months in the job, he wrote a friend, "Columbia is the place I THINK I can do the most good for all—even if that most is a rather pitiful amount."

Dewey's startling defeat by Truman in November 1948 caused Republicans to resume their longing gazes at Eisenhower, although he had succeeded in concealing his party preference from the public. Of a talk with Dewey in July 1949, he wrote, "The governor says that I am a public possession, that such standing as I have in the affections or respect of our citizenry is likewise public property. . . . (Although I'm merely repeating someone else's exposition, the mere writing of such things almost makes me dive under the table). . . . He assumes I am a Republican and would like to be president. (When this last came out I was flabbergasted. I must have had a funny look on my face, because he said, 'I know you disclaimed political ambition in a verbose, wordy document, but that was when you were just a soldier.') This reaffirms a conviction I have formed, which is that no denial of political ambition will ever be believed by a politician, unless the disclaimer is so old he is tottering rapidly to the grave. . . .

"The governor then gave me the reasons he believed that only I (if I should carefully preserve my assets) can save this country from going to hades in the handbasket of paternalism, socialism, dictatorship. . . . His basic reasoning is as follows: All middle-class citizens of education have a common belief that tendencies toward centralization and paternalism must be halted and reversed. No one who voices these views can be elected. . . . Consequently, we must look around for someone of great popularity and who has not frittered away his political assets by taking positive stands against national planning, etc., etc. . . . It all seems unreal and forced to me, but I'm not egotistical enough to give any kind of an irrevocable, arbitrary answer at this moment. . . . Gad, how I wish that both parties had the courage to go out for militant advocacy to the middle of the road and choose some issues outside of the nation's economy on which to fight elections. . . . Oh, yes! Governor said, unless I do something, by 1950, of political significance

Supreme Commander of SHAPE, 1951: Eisenhower reports to the American people on Europe, sees NATO troops in Norway, and reviews American troops with President Truman during a brief visit to Washington. He and Mamie are greeted by John and Barbara Eisenhower and their children Anne and David.

(elected to governorship) I'm through. When I grinned and said, 'You've given me the best of reasons for doing nothing,' he replied, 'Not if you want to preserve democracy.' "

Eisenhower was diverted from his duties at Columbia by Washington and world issues. When the Western democracies joined to form NATO in 1949, Herbert Hoover, Senator Robert Taft of Ohio, and millions of other Americans continued to resist the notion of collective security requiring an American political, military, and economic presence on the European continent. When North Koreans invaded South Korea in June 1950, the United States government girded itself for a possible Soviet attack against Western Europe. "Then the blow!" Eisenhower later wrote. Truman asked him to serve as the first Supreme Commander of NATO's defense forces, negotiating the details of military cooperation with the leaders of Western Europe and preserving the victory won in 1945.

"I do not think it is particularly important where I am working as long as I feel I am doing the best I can in what I definitely believe to be a world crisis," Eisenhower wrote in his October 1950 diary. "It will, of course, be a wrench to give up the work I am so earnestly working on at Columbia, but there are some fine young men there that can carry on. . . . I firmly believe that my own maximum possibilities for service—based upon my alleged prestige in Europe—will begin to diminish very soon after the organizational phases of the proposition

**Congress of the United States**
**House of Representatives**
**Washington, D. C.**

February 22, 1952

General Dwight D. Eisenhower
Supreme Allied Commander, Europe
APO 55, c/o Postmaster
New York, New York

My dear General:

This is a difficult letter to write but it comes to you from the hearts of some of your sincerest friends who have been working for your Presidential candidacy for months. It is prompted by the messages we are receiving daily from our constituents, from all parts of the nation, indicating that they want you to seek the nomination for President of the United States. They want you to come home; they want you to declare yourself on the pressing issues of the day; they want the inspiration of your dynamic honesty and the forthrightness of your statesmanship. The demands of these patriotic Americans have a right to be heard, and we beg you to listen to them because we agree with them.

There can be no doubt that an overwhelming majority of the people of the United States want you as their leader. They realize that for some time you have been devoting your energies to organizing and implementing the defense of Europe, and have accomplished much, but they also realize that if our own country is torn asunder by corruption and greed, by disloyalties and opportunism, by the avarice of selfish men, by the lack of vision of pseudo-statesmen greedy to retain public office, all the good and constructive work you have done will be destroyed. We feel deeply that those basic convictions for which you have stood and which are shared by so many millions of people deserve your personal leadership in this crucial hour. Your return home will unite our people as never before, and this is the surest way to preserve your efforts in Europe and to promote peace in the world.

Before signing this letter we discussed the foreign and domestic situation and your place in it from many angles, and with intense sincerity believe in what is said in this letter. We are practical and not hysterical and venture the thought that perhaps you do not fully appreciate the serious state of our country's domestic affairs. We pledge ourselves to your leadership without thought of any kind of reward -- what we want to do is to save America and promote peace.

With assurances of our high esteem and in the hope of an early and favorable reply,

Sincerely yours,

Clifford R. Hope, Kansas

Hugh D. Scott, Jr., Penna.

Christian A. Herter, Mass.

Winston L. Prouty, Vermont

Claude I. Bakewell, Missouri

James C. Auchincloss, N.J.

Jacob K. Javits, N.Y.

Thruston B. Morton, Kentucky

Edward L. Sittler, Jr., Penna.

Albert M. Cole, Kansas

Gerald R. Ford, Jr., Mich.

Clifford P. Case, N.J.

Thor C. Tollefson, Wash.

John W. Heselton, Mass.

R. Walter Riehlman, N.Y.

W. Sterling Cole, N.Y.

Harmar D. Denny, Jr., Penna.

Norris Cotton, N.H.

Robert W. Kean, N.J.

---

Winter and spring 1952: The presidential campaign begins without the candidate. Nineteen members of Congress implore Eisenhower to run. His campaign manager, Senator Henry Cabot Lodge of Massachusetts, beams after one of the Eisenhower write-in victories in the Republican primaries that had begun with New Hampshire. In Paris in April, as he publicly professes to be noncommittal but has privately decided to run, the General appears convincingly disconcerted by the "I Like Ike" badges affixed to photographers' cameras.

begin to show results. We must remember that the whole scheme may be one that will have to remain in effect for ten, fifteen, or twenty years." He wrote his Abilene friend Swede Hazlett, "I rather look upon this effort as about the last remaining chance for the survival of Western civilization."

Taft was the Republican presidential frontrunner for 1952. Before seeing him on the eve of his trip to Paris, Eisenhower wrote out a statement that would "kill off any further speculation about me as a candidate for the Presidency," and offered to issue it if Taft would support NATO and collective security. The Ohio Senator refused. After he departed, Eisenhower tore up his statement and decided to retain his leverage by keeping "an aura of mystery" about his plans for 1952.

By now Republicans had been shut out of the White House and congressional leadership for two decades. Even against the unbeloved Harry Truman—and with Wallace and the Dixiecrat Governor Strom Thurmond of South Carolina draining millions of normally Democratic votes—Dewey had lost. If the 1952 convention should choose Taft, who would probably lose the crucial independent vote, Democratic dominance might be extended to 1961. But Republican leaders could only presume that Eisenhower generally approved of Truman's approach to foreign affairs. They knew little of where he stood on domestic issues and could not even be certain that he was a Republican. (*McCall's* offered him $40,000 to answer the question, "Are you a

Republican?") Nevertheless, many looked on him now as their only savior.

In the summer of 1951, a Citizens for Eisenhower group was formed by the General's friends among New York business and finance, led by William Robinson of the *New York Herald Tribune*, organ of northeastern Republicanism. In September, Senator Henry Cabot Lodge of Massachusetts went to Paris and told Eisenhower that the election would be a cinch: The nomination would be the hard part. If the General did not allow his name to be used in Republican primaries, Taft would sew it up.

In his October diary, Eisenhower wrote with at least the partial motive of impressing future historians with his lack of hunger for the Presidency: "The temptation grows to issue a short, definite statement saying no (in almost arbitrary language). If I wanted to be president I'd resign today and start traveling the United States about January 1. But the personal belief that I could do a good job would have to be so strong as to make me feel justified in leaving this onerous and strenuous post of duty. . . . Of course, because of the remote, very remote, possibility that persons may, in spite of my silence, succeed in producing a grassroots draft, I have to think more about the subject than is involved merely in a negative attitude. When people like Paul Hoff-

man, Governors Dewey and Stassen, Senators Duff, Carlson, Lodge, etc., great friends like [Lucius] Clay, [Mark] Clark, [Roy] Roberts, etc., etc., and others like Craig (American Legion commander of last year) all begin to assert that I have a duty, it is not easy to just say NO."

Eisenhower's brother Milton told him that if the 1952 nominees were likely to be Taft and Truman, then "any personal sacrifice on the part of any honest American citizen is wholly justified." Lodge warned the General in December that he had to return and run, or "the whole effort is hopeless." Eisenhower refused. He did not wish to picture himself as doing anything other than accepting the call of duty. He also knew that "the seeker is never so popular as the sought. People want what they think they can't get."

In January 1952, Lodge entered Eisenhower's name in the New Hampshire primary. He baldly announced that Eisenhower was a Republican and would accept the nomination if offered. Furious, the General wrote in his diary, "Time and time again I've told anyone who'd listen that I will not seek a nomination. I don't give a d— how impossible a 'draft' may be. I'm willing to go part way in trying to recognize a 'duty,' but I do not have to seek one, and I will not." Still, his public response was far more equivocal: Lodge and his men had the right "to place before me next July a duty that would transcend my present responsibility." Eisenhower was further aroused when Truman issued

June 1952: The Eisenhowers return from Paris to Washington. Resigning from the Army, he grimly goes to the White House to see President Truman, for whom he is now a partisan opponent. (Eisenhower's brother Milton stands behind and slightly to the left of Mamie.)

June 1952: Another homecoming to Abilene. Seven years after his return in the wake of VE-Day, Eisenhower's hometown is turned into a minor version of Hollywood on Academy Awards night to welcome the presidential candidate. Watching the parade down the main street from the same balcony on which he had stood in 1945, he and Mamie enjoy a replica of the Eisenhower forebears' 1878 arrival in Abilene—and of their own wedding. Eisenhower and his brother Milton lay the cornerstone for the Eisenhower Museum adjoining the family homestead. This was a splendid piece of timing: No one needed to be reminded that there was no Robert Taft or Adlai Stevenson Museum. He speaks to a rain-drenched crowd.

a budget that was $14 billion in deficit and when Taft demanded that American troops be returned from Europe.

In February, the aviator Jacqueline Cochran came to the Eisenhowers' living room outside Paris and showed them a film of a Madison Square Garden rally. Fifteen thousand people had waved banners and chanted "I like Ike!" for two hours after midnight. After the lights were turned back on, she raised her glass and called out, "To the President!" She recalled that "tears were just running out of his eyes, he was so overwhelmed," and that he talked "about his mother, his father and his family, but mostly about his mother."

Eisenhower wrote Hazlett the next day that the film "brought home to me for the first time something of the depth of the longing in Americans today for a change." Viewing it had been an "emotional experience for Mamie and me. I've not been so upset in years. Clearly to be seen is the mass longing of America for some kind of reasonable solution for her nagging, persistent, and almost terrifying problems. It's a real experience to realize that one could become a symbol of many thousands of the hope they have." Before Cochran left, he said to her, "You can go tell Bill Robinson that I'm going to run."

Late in the spring, he told a reporter, "I'm going to fight like hell for the nomination." In June, timed to coincide with the anniversary of D-Day, Eisenhower returned to Abilene for his first major campaign appearance. A newspaper brayed, "IKE IS BACK IN KANSAS." Of his entry into politics, he told the press, "I hope I never get pontifical or stuffed-shirty with you fellows, but I'm doing this because I feel that I should." He laid the cornerstone for the new Eisenhower Museum next to his boyhood home, then watched a parade whose floats depicted the great events of his life.

In Eisenhower Park, he gave a nationally televised speech before a rain-soaked crowd: "We are, of course, experiencing today a Kansas shower, but I assure you there's not half as much water here today as there was in the English Channel eight years ago today. Moreover, in Kansas we can use this rain—it's okay by me." Devised to allay the fears of the party's Taft wing, the address foreshadowed the campaign. The General deplored inflation, excessive taxation, Big Government, unbalanced budgets, corruption, the secrecy of Yalta, the loss of China ("a tragedy that must not be repeated"), and the danger of permanent one-party domination of the government. Isolationism was "utter futility," but "we should know what is expected of other nations which are expecting help from us, and we should be assured that those programs do not bring about an economic chaos that would defeat us all. . . . A bankrupt America would mean the loss of all we hold dear and would leave much of the world almost naked in front of the Kremlin menace."

Through the spring, Republican primaries had demonstrated Eisenhower's popularity, but delegate strength remained with party rank-and-file and leaders whom Taft had cultivated for years. The lesson they had taken from Dewey's defeat was that it was futile to try

At his newly purchased and unrenovated Gettysburg farm, Eisenhower courts Pennsylvania delegates to the Republican Convention.

July 1952: Betraying his nervousness that this convention might hand him his first major defeat, Eisenhower arrives in Chicago with Milton and Mamie. After the balloting, he calls on Senator Taft. On the convention platform *(opposite)*, he jokes with his selection for Vice President, Senator Richard Nixon of California (still wearing his badge of support for Governor Earl Warren), and greets the delegates.

to capture the center. At the start of the Chicago convention, one poll predicted that Taft would claim 530 delegates against Eisenhower's 427. Eisenhower supporters charged that politicians backing Taft had "stolen" such states as Texas in the face of popular support for the General.

Shrewdly, Lodge proposed and won passage of a "Fair Play Amendment" whose effective result was that both the Eisenhower and other camps combined to stop Taft by seating Eisenhower delegates. Quietly informed that he was being considered for an Eisenhower ticket, Senator Richard Nixon of California warned that if the party gave contested seats to Taft, it would lose the corruption issue and limit its "membership to the minority." In an angry caucus, he took control of his state's delegation from its favorite son, Governor Earl Warren, and gained votes for Eisenhower. With the help of Fair Play and his handlers' other wily maneuvers, the General won the nomination on the first ballot. But when someone proposed that the choice be

made unanimous, Taft diehards shouted, "No!"

For Vice President, Eisenhower's advisors suggested that he select a prominent anti-communist, an energetic, young campaigner who would offset the General's age, a Westerner to offset Eisenhower's links to Dewey and New York finance. First on the list was the thirty-nine-year-old Nixon, who had already gained national fame for his successful pursuit of the espionage case against the American diplomat Alger Hiss. Although twenty-three years older, and despite the fact that he had never had an extended private talk with Nixon, the General nonetheless ratified the selection.

Accepting the nomination, Eisenhower reminded the delegates of his own special qualifications for the Presidency: "I know something of the solemn responsibilities of *leading* a crusade. I *have led* one." Thunderous applause. ". . . I accept your summons. I will *lead* this crusade!"

When Democrats nominated Governor Adlai Stevenson of Illinois, they made the contest one between candidates who would have preferred and might have expected other autumn opponents—Truman and Taft. As the campaign began, Eisenhower had to assuage Taft and his supporters, still angry about what many of them called the "theft" of the Chicago nomination.

Thus he publicly demanded "liberation of the satellite countries" of Eastern Europe, although by "peaceful means." He did not dissuade Nixon from serving as his Doberman, famously attacking Stevenson as a graduate of the "College of Cowardly Communist Containment" led by the Truman Secretary of State, Dean Acheson. Eisenhower invited Taft to a well-publicized breakfast after which the Senator announced that they had reached accord: The real issue was "creeping socialization," and their foreign policy differences were only of degree because they were both "determined" to battle foreign and domestic

The opponent: At the Democratic Convention in Chicago, Governor Adlai Stevenson, standing with the President about whose public support he was so ambivalent.

communism. Stevenson quipped that Taft may have "lost the nomination but won the nominee."

Eisenhower knew how close the Republican Old Guard had come to defeating him in Chicago. For the rest of his life in politics, he was hence more anxious than he probably needed to be about its ability to cause him harm. In 1952, this anxiety took him into scenes he found distasteful and which, had he known they were in his future, might have caused him to think twice about seeking the Presidency. In mid-September, he appeared with Indiana Senator William Jenner, who had called George Marshall a "front man for traitors" and a "living lie." Eisenhower refrained from mentioning Jenner's name and was appalled when Jenner grabbed his arm and raised it high for photographers ("I felt dirty from the touch of the man"), but the damage to his reputation for being above low politics had been done.

In October, Eisenhower was scheduled to appear with Wisconsin Senator Joseph McCarthy, then at the peak of his reckless *jihad* against communists in government. Especially after the Jenner episode, Eisenhower's advisors were eager for him to defend Marshall in McCarthy's presence; they let reporters know that the candidate planned to declare in Milwaukee that charging Marshall with disloyalty was "the way freedom must not defend itself." But under pressure from Wisconsin Republicans and noting that he had already defended Marshall four times in the campaign, Eisenhower agreed to drop the paragraph. He lacked the sensitivity of a more experienced politician to how the public would interpret such a move. The incident shocked even some of the General's supporters, who wondered whether he was so cowed by McCarthy that he would not use his unassailable prestige to cut the demagogue down to size. In the *Washington Post,* the cartoonist Herblock drew a panel labeled "ANYTHING TO WIN."

And there was the Checkers episode. The *New York Post* revealed that a group of California millionaires had started an eighteen-thousand-dollar fund to augment Nixon's Senate salary. This practice was not uncommon at the time but stood in sharp contrast to Nixon's complaints about "corrupt" Truman officials who had taken freezers and mink coats. Many in Eisenhower's circle recommended that Nixon be fired from the ticket. Eisenhower advised him to go on television and tell "everything there is to tell." Then he would wait three or four days to see the effect of the speech. Impatient, Nixon demanded an immediate decision: "There comes a time in matters like this when you've either got to shit or get off the pot." The General was hardly accustomed to being addressed in such fashion.

During Nixon's emotional broadcast, noting his daughters' receipt of a gift dog they named Checkers ("regardless of what they say about it, we're going to keep it"), he called on all candidates to reveal their financial histories as he had. Eisenhower was watching in Cleveland. Determined to keep his privacy, sensitive about his income from *Crusade in Europe* and gifts and favors accepted since the war, when he heard Nixon's demand for full disclosure, his face reddened and he stabbed his pencil into a legal pad. Eisenhower's willingness to let Nixon hang for days out to dry, Nixon's demands, his success in painting Eisenhower into a financial corner, and the independent national constituency his ordeal and television speech now won for him —especially among conservatives—all forever shadowed the two men's relationship. But Nixon stayed on the ticket.

Using an airplane and his "Look Ahead, Neighbor" special train, Eisenhower traveled 51,276 miles through 45 states and 232 towns and cities. A junior aide marveled at his ability to make "sophisticated use of the unsophisticated side of himself." The General once said, "When the people are waving at you, wave your arms and move your lips so you look like you're talking to them. It doesn't matter what you say. Let them see you're reacting to them." In late October, he suggested that intervention by the hero of World War II could end the stalemated

Senator Joseph McCarthy of Wisconsin.

THIS AMERICAN FAITH REFLECTS OUR RESPECT FOR THE IDEALS OF OUR FOUNDERS; OUR PRIDE IN OUR OWN PAST; OUR CONVICTION THAT AMERICA--

Eisenhower thought it a "sad fate for an old soldier" to submit himself to Madison Avenue, but submit he did. Ben Duffy, president of Batten, Barton, Durstine & Osborn, persuaded the General to trade steel-rimmed for horn-rimmed spectacles and to allow himself to be made up for television appearances. Duffy later said that his firm frankly merchandised Eisenhower's honesty, integrity, sincerity, wholesomeness. Commercials were run using the jingle: "I like Ike, you like Ike, everybody likes Ike . . . Let's send Ike to Washington." But unlike later candidates and Presidents, Eisenhower forbade intrusion of campaign technicians into matters of policy.

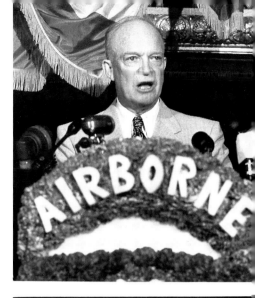

The candidate whistle-stops aboard his "Look Ahead, Neighbor" special.

Speaking to veterans of the 82nd Airborne about the casualties of World War II, Eisenhower breaks down.

two-year-old war in Korea: If elected, "I shall go to Korea." Stevenson had been rising in the polls, but this pledge stopped his ascent. One reporter now packed up his typewriter and went home, saying that the campaign was over.

On election night, Eisenhower went to the ballroom of the Commodore Hotel in New York to accept victory. He was elected with 55.1 percent of the popular vote and 442 electoral votes, including five states in the traditional Democratic Solid South. Stevenson won 44.4 percent and 89 electoral votes, from West Virginia and eight Deep South states. The House and Senate went Republican.

The American people had provided Eisenhower with an unquestionable mandate to be President, but what kind of President was not so clear. He had left it an open question whether he would use the Presidency to convert a set of beliefs into law or principally to reign and unify. With those who voted for him divided mainly between the right and the center, it was unclear whether he would pursue liberation of the Soviet bloc or a Truman-style containment, repeal the New Deal or revise and manage it more efficiently.

Eisenhower was the first President since another victorious General, Ulysses Grant, to be elected without previous political experience. Through the Army years and afterward, he had developed a mastery of bureaucratic politics, foreign and defense strategy, and worked alongside difficult leaders from MacArthur to Montgomery. But he was a novice in party and congressional politics and the complex art of appealing to an electorate for support of his policies. Choosing him mainly for his wartime achievements and the kind of man he was, Americans had opted for a greater experiment than they probably knew.

Election night, 1952, the Commodore Hotel, New York.

November 1952: Fulfilling his campaign pledge, the President-elect goes to Korea. Harry Truman had intensified the bitterness of their political break by wiring Eisenhower after the election to offer him a government plane "if" he still planned to visit Korea. Eisenhower considered this an insult to his integrity, as if the promise had been simply something to be tossed off and forgotten after the election.

# 4.
# MANDATE

My first day at the president's desk," Eisenhower wrote in his diary on January 21, 1953. "Plenty of worries and difficult problems. But such has been my portion for a long time—the result is that this just seems (today) like a continuation of all I've been doing since July 1941—even before that."

He later recalled that the country was "in an unhappy state. There was bitterness and there was quarrelling. . . . I tried to create an atmosphere of greater serenity and confidence."

With the stalemate in Korea and Stalin in the final stages of his dementia, the Cold War had almost never been more frigid. In the years after VE-Day, Eisenhower had been one of the last to relinquish the dream of genuine collaboration between Washington and Moscow. Testifying before the House Military Affairs Committee in 1945, he said, "Russia has not the slightest thing to gain by a struggle with the United States. There is no thing, I believe, that guides the policy of Russia more today than to keep friendship with the United States." He had hoped for a postwar world without hostile alliances or arms races, in which nuclear weapons would be under the control of the United Nations: When the atomic bomb was first tested, his response was "a feeling of depression."

During the presidential campaign, the Republican Right had recalled Eisenhower's failure to take Berlin in 1945 and his cheerful postwar talk about the Russians. This had compelled him to stress his warnings to Western leaders during and after the war about the Soviet danger and to issue his promise that, as President, he would never recognize Soviet domination of Eastern Europe. Nonetheless he disappointed the more strenuous anticommunists in his party with his insistence that the Iron Curtain would be rolled back without force.

In March 1953, Stalin died. His heir apparent, Georgi Malenkov, surprised Washington by saying, "There is not one disputed or undecided question that cannot be decided by peaceful means." The new President told his new Secretary of State,

Eisenhower Rex.

January 20, 1953: On inaugural morning, still indignant toward Truman, Eisenhower followed custom by driving to the White House to pick up the outgoing President on the way to inaugural ceremonies at the Capitol but broke it by refusing to go inside to escort Truman to the car. Posing with Eisenhower for photographers, Truman conceals his fury. (Mamie Eisenhower is seen at left between Truman's daughter Margaret and wife, Bess.)

On the White House inaugural stand, Eisenhower allows himself to be lassoed by a cowboy in the inaugural parade. (At right are the new First Lady and Vice President.) That evening, the Eisenhowers walk into the White House for the first time during the Eisenhower Presidency.

John Foster Dulles, "Look, I am tired—and I think everyone is tired—of just plain indictments of the Soviet regime. I think it would be wrong—in fact, asinine—for me to get up before the world now to make another one of those indictments."

In April, before the American Society of Newspaper Editors in Washington, Eisenhower gave the best speech of his life. Welcoming Malenkov's offer, he pledged that when it was backed by deeds, he would join the Soviets to limit arms and place atomic energy under international control. His most imperishable passage evoked the price of an eternal arms race:

"Every gun that is fired, every warship launched, every rocket fired signifies . . . a *theft* from those who hunger and are not fed, those who are cold and not clothed. This world in arms is not spending money alone. It is spending the sweat of its laborers, the genius of its scientists, the hopes of its children. . . . We pay for a single fighter plane with a half million bushels of wheat. We pay for a single destroyer with new homes that could have housed more than eight thousand people. This is not a way of life at all, in any true sense. Under the cloud of threatening war, it is humanity hanging from a cross of iron."

As the speech, called "The Chance for Peace," showed, Eisenhower's second greatest fear about the arms race was that the two societies would spend themselves into oblivion. His first was that some American or Soviet leader, faced with this prospect, might try to destroy the threat with a surprise nuclear attack. This he considered the most urgent reason for disarmament. "As of now," he wrote in his diary, "the world is racing toward catastrophe."

At the United Nations in December 1953, he proposed a plan that

The "abominable no man": Sherman Adams, the former Governor of New Hampshire whom Eisenhower had appointed Assistant to the President, in which role he exercised considerable power. During his first year, Eisenhower wrote in his diary that "honesty, directness and efficiency" had begun to win Adams "friends among people who initially were prone to curse him because he had no time for flattery or cajolery, or even pleasantries over the telephone."

During a Cabinet meeting, Eisenhower is bemused by his Secretary of State, John Foster Dulles. (Behind him is his first Defense Secretary, Charles Wilson, former chief of General Motors.) Dulles's prominence as a spokesman and his willingness to take the heat for unpopular policies led many to suppose that he, not the President, was the chief arbiter of the Eisenhower approach to the world. This canard was corrected by later historians.

Senator William Knowland of California, who became Eisenhower's party leader in the Senate after the death of Robert Taft in July 1953. The President privately considered Knowland a symbol of the right-wing Republicanism with which he had to deal throughout his Presidency. He wrote in his diary that in Knowland's case, there seemed to be no final answer to the question, "How stupid can you get?"

Soviet Premier Georgi Malenkov *(fourth from left),* Stalin's immediate successor, standing with other members of the post-Stalin leadership including Nikita Khrushchev *(third from right).*

became known as "Atoms for Peace": "Today, the United States stockpile of atomic weapons, which, of course, increases daily, exceeds by many times the explosive equivalent of the total of all bombs and all shells that came from every plane and every gun in every theater of war in all the years of World War II." Unless the arms race ended, the "two atomic colossi" would be doomed to "eye each other indefinitely across a trembling world." He proposed that the United States, Britain, and Soviet Union make contributions from their nuclear stockpiles to a UN atomic agency for peaceful uses.

This would curb the arms race at an early stage without requiring the inspections of nuclear sites that the Russians opposed. The President knew that the United States could reduce its stockpile by several times the Soviet rate and remain superior: His speech suggested that the ratio of American to Soviet contributions might be five to one or more. The Soviets refused the plan, unwilling to brook a possibly permanent American lead. Nevertheless, at a time when others merely presumed an eternal American-Soviet military competition (including many of his own appointees, who took a faintly patronizing attitude toward his optimism), Eisenhower kept alive the hope that Atoms for Peace or some other first step would be one first "chip in the granite" of the Cold War.

Stalin's death and Malenkov's offer to settle outstanding questions may have persuaded the Chinese that they might not be able to rely forever on Soviet weaponry in the Korean War. In the spring of 1953, at the President's behest, Foster Dulles told the Indian government that the United States might be forced to use its full arsenal. Nuclear warheads were moved to forward bases in Okinawa. At the heretofore stagnant talks on Korea, the Chinese quickly accepted an American proposal for a prisoner exchange. In July, an armistice was signed. We do not know whether the principal motivation for the change was Stalin's death, Dulles's threats, or the more general feeling in Beijing that Eisenhower would be less patient or restrained than Truman in allowing the conflict to grind on.

Committed to both fiscal prudence and military strength, Eisenhower authorized defense cuts under a program dubbed the "New Look." Conventional forces were reduced by six divisions, the Navy by less; air power was to be increased by thirty thousand men and twenty-two wings. Under the new doctrine, deployment of tactical nuclear weapons would be considered for local wars, but the chief American retaliatory response in crisis would be the unpredictable use of massive nuclear force against the Soviet Union or China. The

Earl Warren of California, whom Eisenhower appointed Chief Justice in 1953. He later objected to Warren's judicial activism.

strength of "massive retaliation" was that it saved money; the chief defect was that the more the bluff was employed, the less it would work, not to mention the danger that it would trigger a tragic chain of superpower escalation that could culminate in actual nuclear war. Its use was further limited by Western European allies who feared Soviet retaliation and world condemnation.

In the spring of 1954, despite millions of dollars in American aid, France was losing control of Vietnam to nationalist communist guerrillas led by Ho Chi Minh. During the Battle of Dien Bien Phu, the French argued that American military aid was essential to strengthen their hand in negotiations at Geneva. Admiral Arthur Radford, Chairman of the Joint Chiefs of Staff, proposed that sixty B-29 bombers run night raids along the perimeter around Dien Bien Phu. Eisenhower refused to sanction the idea unless approved by Congress and other Western allies: "Without allies and associates, the leader is just an adventurer, like Genghis Khan." The British refused. Having avoided war with China over Korea, with the benefit of United Nations support, the President had no desire to provoke another, this time standing alone.

As for brandishing the Bomb, Eisenhower later recalled telling his staff, "You boys must be crazy. We can't use those awful things against Asians for the second time in less than ten years." The historian of nuclear weapons McGeorge Bundy has concluded that American possession of thermonuclear weapons probably "increased the appeal of a peaceful result for the Russians and perhaps also the Chinese." The talks at Geneva achieved a truce that was to lead to a political settlement that did not come. Eisenhower committed the United States to the Southeast Asia Treaty Organization, which compelled it to preserve an independent South Vietnam, but he succeeded in keeping American ground forces out of the country, as his three successors did not.

These years saw a large increase in the resources and license of the

Central Intelligence Agency. The President wrote a friend in 1955, "I have come to the conclusion that some of our traditional ideas of international sportsmanship are scarcely applicable in the morass in which the world now founders. Truth, honesty, justice, consideration for others, liberty for all—the problem is how to preserve them, nurture them and keep the peace (if the last is possible) when we are opposed by people who scorn these values."

In 1953, he ordered the Agency to collaborate with British intelligence against Mohammed Mossadegh, the Iranian Prime Minister whose nationalization of Western oil interests had brought on an international boycott of Iranian oil. In May, Mossadegh asked Eisenhower to help end the boycott, leading Washington to suppose that otherwise he would ask for Soviet aid. As Mossadegh increased his grip on Iran, Shah Mohammed Reza Pahlevi departed the country. The CIA and British secret service responded with Operation Ajax, which restored the Shah to his throne and near-absolute authority as a firm Western ally. Mossadegh was deposed and thrown on trial. The next year, in Guatemala, President Jacobo Arbenz Guzman expropriated unculti-vated lands of the American-based United Fruit Company under a land reform program which some in Washington took as the first step toward Marxism. CIA-trained mercenaries marched toward Guatemala City. As Agency pilots bombed the capital, Arbenz fled and a pro-American military junta took power.

After the Korean armistice, Eisenhower's first term was chiefly domestic. Despite the career spent on matters of national security, the thirty-fourth President came to office with a philosophy of domestic affairs that was more considered than most of the voters who elected him had perceived. More than any other twentieth-century President, he adhered to the idealistic view of human nature held particularly during the period after Independence—the belief that the New World citizen was a New Man (in Crèvecoeur's phrase) endowed with special capacities for rational thought, self-discipline, self-sacrifice, and that Americans' affection for their new, hard-won society would ensure subordination of private interests to the country's good.

Few Presidents since Washington have been very confident about persuading Americans to make serious sacrifices in the absence of war or other national emergency. It was the failure of Franklin Roosevelt's efforts to orchestrate business-government cooperation during the worst of the Depression that pushed him toward special interest brokerage during the Second New Deal of the late 1930s.

Eisenhower was different. He had matured in a community whose citizens looked after one another. He had risen in an Army where ambition was muted and subordinated to team and nation. As Supreme Commander, hour by hour he had made decisions whose literal consequences had been life and death, war and peace. Before reaching the White House, a Roosevelt or a Truman was exposed to the full blast of partisan greed and selfishness. Eisenhower's extraordinary experience made him far more hopeful than a veteran politician that a President

Covert action in Iran and Guatemala.

Iran, September 1953 *(above, left and right):* The CIA helps to depose Prime Minister Mohammed Mossadegh and bring near-absolute power to the young Shah of Iran. Mossadegh is tried and imprisoned.

Guatemala, June 1954: Another CIA-inspired coup removes the left-leaning President Jacobo Arbenz Guzman *(second from left).*

could ask congressmen, labor leaders, bankers, defense manufacturers, or lobbyists to restrain the pursuit of their own interests in service of a long-range vision of the good of the country. Eisenhower wrote a friend, "To induce people to do more, leadership has the chore of informing people and inspiring them to real sacrifice." This was near the center of his aspiration to be less a Roosevelt than a Washington, a unifying figure above partisan politics whose conspicuous patriotism and devotion to the long-term national interest would endow him with special powers of healing and persuasion.

Eisenhower's years of private railleries against the "paternalism" and "statism" of the New Deal and afterwards did not go for naught. He reduced government regulation of business, removed wage and price controls, gave control of tideland undersea oil reserves to individual states and industry, blocked expansion of the Tennessee Valley Authority. But he disappointed the Taft wing of his party by refusing to call for repeal of Social Security, the minimum wage, or other highly popular legacies of Democratic rule. From the end of the Truman years through the Eisenhower Presidency, the percentage of the national budget that went to transfer payments actually increased. As Eisenhower wrote his brother Edgar, he knew that "should any political party attempt to abolish Social Security, unemployment insurance, and eliminate labor laws and farm programs, you would not hear of that party again in our political history."

In harmony with his own party, he was concerned more about inflation than unemployment: He tolerated sluggish growth and recession rather than surrender without a fight to unbalanced budgets. Less allergic to the power of the corporation than that of the state, he brought businessmen into government as never before. Antitrust action was relaxed. Under a President calling for cooperation between business and government, public-private advisory councils were appointed to study national problems such as housing, nuclear power production, and the federal highway system. The result of the last was Eisenhower's Interstate Highway Act, which authorized construction of more than forty thousand miles of four-, six-, and eight-lane controlled-access roads, forming the backbone of the world's most comprehensive highway network.

The President's insistence on remaining above partisan politics was tested soon after his inauguration by Joseph McCarthy. As during the 1952 campaign, Eisenhower avoided open confrontation with the Wisconsin demagogue. He did not wish to drag his office into the mud, give the senator more publicity, and further polarize the country. Nor did he wish to inflame Republican conservatives who still had their doubts about Eisenhower. He wrote Swede Hazlett, "Whenever the President takes part in a newspaper trial of some individual of whom he disapproves, one thing is automatically accomplished. This is an increase in the headline value of the individual attacked." He told his brother Milton more bluntly, "I just won't get into a pissing contest with that skunk."

His April 1953 diary: "Senator McCarthy is, of course, so anxious for the headlines that he is prepared to go to any extremes in order to secure some mention of his name in the public press. His actions create trouble on the Hill with members of the party; they irritate, frustrate, and infuriate members of the Executive Department. I really believe that nothing will be so effective in combating his particular kind of troublemaking as to ignore him. This he cannot stand."

Instead, Eisenhower strove to preempt the issue of anticommunism. He approved laws to strip citizenship from Americans planning violent overthrow of the government, forcing witnesses to surrender Fifth Amendment protection during investigations involving national security, broadening statutes against espionage and sabotage. A new internal security review program allowed government employees to be fired not only for disloyalty but "unsuitability." He approved the revocation of a high-security clearance from the physicist J. Robert Oppenheimer while privately conceding that there was little evidence to justify it. He refused to prevent the convicted spies Julius and Ethel Rosenberg from execution because the "exemplary feature of the punishment" was "the hope that it would deter others." At the State Department, he and Foster Dulles approved the appointment of Scott McLeod, a McCarthy confederate, as Chief of Security and Consular Affairs, in which capacity McLeod mowed through the professional Foreign Service in search of communists.

In November 1953, Eisenhower's perceptive and devoted secretary, Ann Whitman, wondered whether the administration's effort to take the anticommunist issue away from McCarthy had gone too far. As she recorded in her diary, she gave the President "information that people were critical of impression Foster Dulles was making with especial reference to damage of prestige abroad and to bad morale in

Joseph McCarthy with his pugnacious counsel Roy Cohn during the Army-McCarthy hearings. Eisenhower wrote in his April 1953 diary that McCarthy's actions "create trouble on the Hill" and "irritate, frustrate and infuriate" members of the Executive Branch: "I really believe that nothing will be so effective in combating his particular kind of troublemaking as to ignore him. This he cannot stand."

Ho Chi Minh of Vietnam. Eisenhower kept American forces out in 1954 but sowed some of the seeds of later involvement.

foreign service. He worried the matter over the weekend; cannot see that criticism is justified. Criticism does hurt him, makes him unhappy —trying to make him see it is the fringe element, the columnists that are trying to make trouble—that the people on the street believe in him just as much as they ever did."

In 1954, as McCarthy's attack progressed from the Truman to the Eisenhower administration, the President moved more openly against McCarthy and his methods. Before McCarthy began his much-bally-hooed investigation of the U. S. Army, Eisenhower supported Army counteraccusations against the Senator and had his press secretary, James Hagerty, pass to reporters information and questions intended to damage the Senator. Asserting the doctrine of executive privilege (providing a fateful precedent twenty years later during President Richard Nixon's Watergate scandal), the President refused to hand over to Congress records of meetings between officials of the Executive Branch and the Army. After the Senator finally wounded himself in the infamous Army-McCarthy hearings, Eisenhower encouraged Republicans to vote for the censure resolution that in December 1954 ended McCarthy's national career. McCarthy struck back by accusing the President of "weakness and supineness" against communists and apologized to the American people for supporting Eisenhower in 1952. But by then, few were listening.

The President's partisans at the time and later historians praised his dexterity in undermining McCarthy without jeopardizing his support by the Right or involving himself in an ugly, diminishing fight with a demagogue. But as others fairly argued, Eisenhower's approach also cost reputations and lives. It failed to fulfill the presidential duty of moral leadership and evinced less sensitivity to civil liberties than to more temporal political priorities.

Eager to retain control of the Congress, Eisenhower was alarmed in October 1954 when polls showed a Democratic surge. Worried that if Congress was lost, the right-wing Old Guard would try to recapture the party, he scrapped his intention to differentiate himself from Truman by keeping the Presidency out of the midterm campaign. Eisenhower's almost forty political speeches and ten thousand miles of political travel failed to reverse the tendency for Presidents to lose seats in off-year elections. The House and Senate reverted to the Democrats. The President told Hagerty, "I have just one purpose, outside of the job of keeping this world at peace, and that is to build up a strong progressive Republican party in this country. . . . If the right wing wants a fight, they're going to get it. If they want to leave the Republican party and form a third party, that's their business, but before I end up, either this Republican party will reflect progressivism or I won't be with them any more."

Since Truman and Stalin at Potsdam in 1945, no American President had sat in the same room as his Soviet counterpart. During 1953, Winston Churchill, once again British Prime Minister, had pleaded for a new East-West meeting, but Eisenhower and Dulles worried that

The midterm campaign of 1954: Eisenhower tries and fails to preserve Republican majorities in the House and Senate. At bottom he speaks to a rally in the Hollywood Bowl.

June 1955: Eisenhower attends the fortieth reunion of the Class of 1915 at West Point, along with General Omar Bradley *(at left, legs crossed)*. The same month, while leaving the Oval Office to go to the Mansion for a cocktail, he is rushed away for a civil defense exercise rehearsing continuity of presidential leadership during a nuclear attack *(opposite)*. He had insisted on not knowing exactly when or how this exercise would be staged so that it would be more realistic. With his staff secretary and close aide, General Andrew Goodpaster, looking over his shoulder, he signs documents at the underground presidential command center.

such talks might diminish the sense of national urgency required to build NATO. At a time when McCarthy was still potent and the President still building his credentials with conservatives, Eisenhower was reluctant to allow his enemies to charge him with practicing appeasement behind closed doors.

By 1955, these worries had faded. The post-Stalin leadership struggle seemed to be ending: Malenkov had given way to a duumvirate composed of Prime Minister Nikolai Bulganin and Communist Party leader Nikita Khrushchev, who might now have the authority to bargain seriously on arms control and disarmament. At a press conference, the President suggested that if the Russians showed some sign of earnestness, such as a treaty removing East and West occupation troops from Austria, he would lift his objection to a summit. The Soviets agreed. An American-Soviet-British-French meeting was scheduled for Geneva in mid-July. Before leaving Washington with Mamie and John on the presidential plane *Columbine III,* Eisenhower felt compelled to assure congressional leaders that Geneva would not be another Yalta.

Arriving at Geneva, he said, "Eleven years ago, I came to Europe with an army, a navy and an air force. This time I come with something more powerful . . . the aspirations of Americans for peace." Over dinner, ignoring Foster Dulles's counsel to keep an "austere countenance" while Russians were present, the President said it was

July 1955, the Geneva summit: Eisenhower, Soviet Premier Nikolai Bulganin, French Premier Edgar Faure, and British Premier Anthony Eden arrive for a picture session in front of the Palais des Nations. The huge table, cavernous meeting room, and number of spectators impede serious progress to end the Cold War. When Eisenhower returns to Washington in the rain, Vice President Nixon orders the presidential staff not to use umbrellas in order to prevent comparisons between Geneva and Neville Chamberlain's appeasement of Hitler at Munich.

"essential" to "find some way of controlling the threat of the thermo-nuclear bomb. You know, we both have enough weapons to wipe out the entire northern hemisphere from fallout alone." Khrushchev agreed: "We get your dust, you get our dust, the winds blow and nobody's safe."

During three days of formal sessions in the Palais des Nations, Eisenhower challenged the Soviets on the most intractable issues, such as free elections in a unified Germany, Eastern Europe, communist expansionism. Khrushchev insisted that the Germans "have not yet had time to be educated to the great advantage of communism," Bulganin that Soviet "internal affairs" like Eastern Europe were not open for discussion.

On the afternoon of the fourth day, the President took off his glasses, looked at the Russians, and said, "I have been searching my heart and mind for something that I could say here that could convince everyone of the great sincerity of the United States." Under a plan called "Open Skies," he proposed mutual aerial inspection and exchange of blueprints of the military complexes of East and West that could reduce suspicions about military spending and preparation for surprise attack, a deep worry for Eisenhower's generation since Pearl Harbor. Since the Russians knew much more about American facilities than the United States did about theirs, the plan would bring greater benefit to the West. Eisenhower said, "Don't kick the idea out the window." He was trying to "outline one first concrete step" that would show the world their "joint intention not to fight against each other." Khrushchev attacked the plan as a "bald espionage plot."

The summit concluded without concrete achievement but brought the calmest international moment since the start of the Cold War. "Don't worry," Bulganin assured the President before leaving Geneva. "This will come out all right." In London, Foreign Minister Harold Macmillan told reporters, "There ain't gonna be no war." When Eisenhower sent Bulganin a friendly post-summit letter, the Russian replied, "I and my colleagues were deeply touched by your message. . . . After our meeting, we all believe now that in the future, given the existence of goodwill and recognition of mutual interests . . . it will be possible in the final reckoning to guarantee a prolonged and stable peace."

In August, the President and First Lady went to Mamie's family home in Denver for a long vacation. Relaxing with his usual relentlessness, Eisenhower cooked, painted, rode horseback, played bridge and golf, and fished for trout in a rushing stream high in the Rockies. During a golf game late in September, he was called away from the fourteenth green to take a telephone call from Foster Dulles, which he thought unnecessary. The quality of his game collapsed. After eighteen holes, he wolfed down a Salisbury steak with Bermuda onions and returned to the course to vindicate himself. Twice more he was interrupted by calls from Dulles. His longtime doctor and friend, Major General Howard Snyder, noticed that "his anger became so real that the veins stood out on his forehead like whipcords."

Before dawn the next morning, the President was writhing in his bed. His wife said, "What's the matter, Ike? Are you having a nightmare?" Snyder raced to the house in an Air Force car and divined that Eisenhower had suffered a serious heart attack. He gave his patient a pearl of amyl nitrate to sniff and injections of papaverine, morphine, and heparin. The President refused to wear an oxygen mask and "incoherently" insisted on other forms of relief. At Snyder's order, Eisenhower's valet, Sergeant John Moaney, rubbed the President with heated alcohol and wedged hot water bottles about his body, but Eisenhower went into shock. Snyder asked Mamie to wrap her body around her husband for calm and warmth. This worked, and he slept for seven hours.

Only later, after being rushed to Fitzsimons Army Hospital and zipped into an oxygen tent, did the President hear the diagnosis. In Washington, notified of the massive coronary, Richard Nixon cried, "My God!" Two weeks later, when he saw the President in Denver, Eisenhower told him, "I never told Mamie how much it hurt." Released from the hospital in November, the President went to their newly renovated white farmhouse adjoining the battlefield in Gettysburg to convalesce.

Especially at a time when a massive heart attack betokened greater danger than it later did of invalidism or death, the President sank into

Fall 1955: A massive heart attack turns Eisenhower overnight into a depressed semi-invalid. On the roof of his Denver hospital, he is rolled out for his first presentation to reporters *(opposite)*. His press secretary, James Hagerty *(above)*, generally accounted the best presidential spokesman in history, calms the public hysteria with almost excessive disclosure of the President's condition. In November, seen in his bubble-topped limousine, Eisenhower returns east to recuperate in Gettysburg. Leaving the Gettysburg Post Office, where he has established a small temporary office, he doffs his hat to local citizens. Resuming his presidential duties at Camp David, Eisenhower strolls with his naval aide, Captain Edward Beach, and Allen Dulles, Director of Central Intelligence.

depression. Even if he survived, this proud, independent, willful, combustible man faced the prospect of a life stage-managed by doctors and, as Ann Whitman put it, wrapped in "cotton wool." When Eisenhower inveighed against his therapy, Dr. Snyder noticed that he "seemed to be saying to me that he felt I was guilty of a grave error in judgment in not protecting him from this abuse. I never attempted to defend myself. . . . To arouse the President's anger would seem like committing murder to me." Warned to avoid "irritation, frustration, anxiety, fear, and, above all, anger," the patient barked out, "Just what do you think the Presidency *is?*"

A British diplomat wired London: "If Eisenhower does not run, defeat at the Presidential elections seems certain for the Republicans. In that case, the Republican Party would almost certainly find itself at the mercy of its extreme right wing which would mean that it would lose all the gains in policy which Eisenhower's leadership had brought to it." (The diplomat marveled at the publicity about the President's condition: "Even a life insurance agent would hardly demand such complete details of Mr. Eisenhower's health." London replied, "Certainly unusual—but typically American.")

Several months before the heart attack, the President had confided to an aide, Gabriel Hauge, that unless there was some national or international emergency, he did not intend to run again. He said that during his four years in office he had not sought "to complete, but rather to point the way toward a reversal of the trend of the last twenty years and to give the Republican Party a chance to do it." He thought his administration had "encouraged the people of the United States to something other than dependence upon governmental support and subsidies and paternalism." He argued that "a man who is getting to be seventy in the job may be slowing up like the devil."

But he continued to worry that he had not done enough to bring his party toward the center: "The Republican party must be known as a progressive organization or it is sunk. I believe this so emphatically that I think that far from appeasing or reasoning with the dyed-in-the-wool reactionary fringe, we should completely ignore it and when necessary, repudiate it. . . . The political strength that these people could generate in the United States could not elect a man who was committed to giving away twenty-dollar gold pieces to every citizen in the United States for each day of the calendar year. . . . [T]heir thinking is completely uncoordinated with the times in which we live. With them labor is merely an item in their cost sheets, and labor is guilty of effrontery when it questions the wisdom or authenticity of any statement of management or of financiers. They are isolationists who believe that the United States alone could live and prosper in a world gone communist—in which belief they are the most ignorant people now living in the United States. (Possibly I should have taken in more territory.)"

Through December 1955, Eisenhower stalked the grounds at Gettysburg, wondering whether his retirement might mean the victory of

February 1956: Eisenhower emerges from the West Wing of the White House to announce that he will seek a second term. In New York, Republicans watch the President on television. In a letter to his childhood friend Swede Hazlett, Eisenhower explains his reasoning.

March 2, 1956

Personal and Confidential

Dear Swede:

The whole tough business of making up my mind to bow my neck to what seemed to be the inevitable; of then deciding how and when to make my announcement as to a second term; and finally the intensive work of preparing notes from which to speak to the American people, has so occupied my mind and days that I simply had no chance to carry out my hope of writing to you in advance to tell you all about it.

Even the giving of my consent, in 1952, to stand for the Republican nomination was not as difficult as was the decision to lay my name again before than convention. I suppose there are no two people in the world who have more than Mamie and I earnestly wanted, for a number of years, to retire to their home -- a home which we did not even have until a year or so ago.

When I first rallied from my attack of September twenty-fourth, I recall that almost my first conscious thought was "Well, at least this settles one problem for me for good and all."

For five weeks I was not allowed to see a newspaper or to listen to a radio. While, within a matter of a week after I was stricken, I took up the practice of daily meetings with Governor Adams and gradually increased my contacts with other members of the staff and the Administration, the doctors still kept the newspapers away for the reason

While privately exploring possibilities to replace Nixon in 1956, the President briefly flirted with the idea of running with the Democratic Governor of Ohio, Frank Lausche, who was a Catholic: "I'd love to run with a Catholic, if only to test it out." He thought that an Eisenhower-Lausche ticket might also attract millions of Democrats and move the Republican Party toward the center and majority status. But Nixon's persistence prevailed. In April, with Hagerty standing behind him, Nixon announces that he has accepted Eisenhower's public invitation to "chart your own course" and will therefore run for reelection.

the Republican Right. He also considered "what the failing health of a President might do to the office and to the cause for which a whole administration might be working." He told Hagerty, "I just hate to turn this country back into the hands of people like Stevenson, Harriman and Kefauver." On Leap Day, 1956, assured by doctors that his health was sufficient, he declared for reelection. "I really don't know the exact moment when he decided to run again," recalled Hagerty. "But I do know that history was made sometime in those weeks at Gettysburg. It was then that he really faced the sheer, God-awful boredom of not being President."

Now he had to choose a second-term Vice President. Eisenhower admired Nixon's intelligence, energy, and political acuity, but more than once observed that his Vice President "just hasn't grown." He doubted that Nixon, whose chief strength was among conservatives, could ever attract what Eisenhower called the "discerning Democrats" and independents required to make the Republicans a majority party. Especially with his heart condition, he wondered whether Nixon should be first in the line of succession during a second term and thus the most likely 1960 Republican nominee. He suggested that Nixon accept a Cabinet post: Four years at the Pentagon, for instance, might give him executive experience that would be useful if he ran for President. The Vice President did not rise to the bait.

During a private Oval Office meeting with the Republican chairman, Leonard Hall (which the President recorded on a hidden tape

machine), Eisenhower said, "Nixon will never be President. People don't like him." Hall replied that it would be the "easiest thing to get Nixon out of the picture willingly." The President said, "All right. You see him and talk to him, but be very, very gentle." But Nixon refused to commit hari-kiri. The President did not feel strongly enough to insist. Perhaps he worried that a public execution would tarnish his benign image. More likely he worried that if he shed Nixon, the Right would rise up against him and undermine his reelection and second term.

In March 1956, he told reporters that the Vice President should "chart his own course." The following month Nixon went to the Oval Office and said he would be "honored" to run. Eisenhower called Hagerty: "Dick has just told me that he'll stay on the ticket. Why don't you take him out right now and let him tell the reporters himself?" Milton Eisenhower, who discussed the episode with his brother at the time, complained to an historian years later that "a more sensitive man" than Nixon would have taken the hint and left the ticket. "But he wanted to be there. He thought this was his chance to be President." Of the President he served, Nixon recalled in 1990, "He could be so genial, yet so cold."

In June 1956, Eisenhower suffered a serious attack of ileitis and was taken to Walter Reed Army Hospital in Washington for emergency surgery on the blocked intestine. He wrote Hazlett, "My 'innards' have been pictured, described and discussed in the papers, to say nothing of the television and radio, until you, along with many others, must be heartily sick of the whole business." Helping to scotch public anxiety about his fitness for reelection, he made a triumphant visit to Panama.

Eisenhower's ambivalence about Nixon's renomination had not disappeared. For several weeks before the August Republican Convention in San Francisco, he refused to stop his former aide Harold Stassen

June 1956: The presidential health issue is briefly renewed as Eisenhower undergoes surgery for ileitis. After the operation, he is serenaded by an Army band outside his Walter Reed Army Hospital window.

The Eisenhowers and their son and daughter-in-law with (left to right) David, Mary Jean, Anne, and Susan, who were frequent overnight White House visitors. In 1957, John Eisenhower joined his father as assistant staff secretary, working under Andrew Goodpaster.

PEACE
1856  1956
PROSPERITY

August 1956: Coronation at
San Francisco, as Republicans
renominate Eisenhower and
Nixon.

Campaign 1956: Supporters of
Adlai Stevenson on the West
Side of New York take
advantage of the criticism of
Eisenhower as a President not
in control of his job *(opposite,
below)*. Confident of the
outcome, the Republican
candidate and his son attend
the World Series *(opposite,
above)*.

from publicly floating the name of Governor Christian Herter of Massachusetts to keep the vice presidential race open. Stassen publicly argued that Nixon might cost the Republican ticket 4 to 6 percent and control of Congress. But after an uproar from the Vice President's supporters in the party and Congress, many of whom felt more emotional and ideological connection to Nixon than to Eisenhower, the President shut down Stassen's gambit.

His position was enviable as the 1956 campaign began. Americans were enjoying high employment and prosperity, the Korean War was over, the nation was at peace, and, after Geneva, there seemed to be serious hope that the Cold War might be moderated. Stephen Ambrose called it "the best year of the century." Never more beloved by his countrymen, Eisenhower had no intention of repeating the strenuous 1952 campaign: He would instead make four or five television speeches. The Democratic ticket of Stevenson and Senator Estes Kefauver of Tennessee he privately found "the sorriest and weakest pair that ever aspired to the highest office in the land"—especially when Stevenson made a nuclear test ban one of his central issues. Eisenhower

In late October, public attention is diverted to the invasion of Suez and the crushing of the Hungarian revolution by Soviet tanks *(opposite)*.

thought nuclear testing too complex and perilous a subject to bring into a political campaign and refused to discuss it.

In 1956, spurred on by Nikita Khrushchev's Secret Speech against Stalin and his concession that there could be more than one road to socialism, Poles rose up against their government. Demonstrations throughout Hungary brought back to power the liberal Imre Nagy, deposed the previous year by Moscow. At the end of October, Nagy told the Russians that Hungary would withdraw from the Warsaw Pact and declare its neutrality. Soviet tanks rolled in. Despite his 1952 promises about "liberation," Eisenhower refused CIA proposals to airdrop arms and supplies to members of the resistance, encouraged for years by the Voice of America and Radio Free Europe; as for American troops, he noted that Hungary was "as inaccessible as Tibet." Bodies were crushed in the streets of Budapest. Two hundred thousand Hungarians fled to the West.

On October 29, Israeli paratroopers covered by French fighter planes dropped onto the Sinai Desert, the first major step of a British-French-Israeli invasion of Egypt so secret that the United States had not been informed. The French were eager to stanch the flow of Egyptian arms and money to rebels in its colony Algeria, Israel to attack what was then its chief Arab enemy, the British to end Egyptian President Gamal Abdel Nasser's seizure of the Suez Canal. Disgusted by the invasion's colonialist trappings and bad faith, Eisenhower demanded an immediate cease-fire.

The day before the election, British and French paratroopers moved on the Canal, followed by amphibious landings. From Moscow, Premier Bulganin coyly invited the President by public letter to join him in stopping the invasion and threatened to drop nuclear bombs on London and Paris. Eisenhower presumed that the Russians, fearing that the Polish and Hungarian rebellions would begin to dissolve the Warsaw Pact, were hoping to use the Suez crisis to harm NATO: "Those boys are both furious and scared. Just as with Hitler, that makes for the most dangerous state of mind. . . . If those fellows start something, we may have to hit 'em—and, if necessary, with everything in the bucket." If the Soviet air force helped Nasser by attacking the British and French, "we would be in war."

The Eisenhowers voted in Gettysburg. The President improved on his 1952 margin, but Republicans did not regain control of Congress. In Washington that evening, he paced his Sheraton Park Hotel suite, waiting for Stevenson's concession: "What in the name of God is that monkey waiting for? Polishing his prose?" When Stevenson appeared on television, the victor walked away from the screen and said, "I'm just looking for a drink."

Suez ended in cease-fire. America briefly became the hero of Third World leaders who never suspected that Eisenhower would turn his back on his European allies. Americans were brought into the murky politics of the Middle East. At the White House in late November, the President greeted some of the first Hungarian refugees to reach the United States.

E lection night, 1956.

# 5.
# "EMPIRE...
# CRUMBLING"

Early in Eisenhower's second term, black Americans were more than ever resolved to demand their rights. During the first term, presidential orders had integrated the armed forces and public facilities in the national capital. But when *Brown* v. *Board of Education of Topeka* caused the Supreme Court to reconsider whether "separate but equal" black public schools were actually equal to their white counterparts, Eisenhower refrained from pressing for integration.

In May 1954, the Court found that segregated schools were indeed unconstitutional. The President called for racial "cooperation" and nonviolence, but privately said that *Brown* had actually set back the day that American society would be fully integrated.

From the time Eisenhower scorned high school football teammates for refusing to play against a black opponent, his sporadic personal relations with blacks were generally marked by grace and sensitivity. He knew that his was the party of Lincoln. Still, as with civil liberties, he saw his role chiefly in terms of quietly prodding behind the scenes as he publicly sought to preserve national tranquility and unity through controversy. He told aides that while he believed in equal opportunity, he opposed "social mingling."

With *Brown* and the Court's implementation ruling, *Brown II,* a year later, a time of waiting ended. The President supported a moderate voting rights bill sponsored by the Justice Department that passed in August 1957. The following month, federal courts rejected Arkansas's resistance to the integration of Little Rock's Central High School. With no enthusiasm but determined to enforce the law, Eisenhower sent Army paratroopers and National Guardsmen to escort black children into the building. As the struggle for equal rights gathered force in the South and around the country, he was never persuaded that silence was morally

Inauguration, 1957: After taking the oath on the East Front of the Capitol, Eisenhower arrives in front of the White House reviewing stand, where he and Nixon greet the crowds.

indefensible or that deferring presidential initiative now might make the civil rights revolution, when it came, more angry and violent. He asked for and won a stronger voting rights law in 1960 but privately felt that Southern schools would not be genuinely desegregated for at least thirty or forty years.

In October 1957, the Soviet Union launched *Sputnik,* the first man-made earth satellite, into orbit. Eisenhower advised his aides and Cabinet to greet the event with public poise. Hagerty said, "We never thought of our program as one which was in a race with the Russians." The President's chief aide, Sherman Adams, said that the United States wasn't interested in "an outer-space basketball game." Eisenhower had been warned about *Sputnik,* but he had never foreseen how much the achievement might damage the self-confidence of a society that had never questioned since 1945 that it was the strongest and best educated in the world.

Most Americans did not understand that launching a satellite was not the same thing as dropping a bomb on a target. Many now made the mistake of supposing that Moscow had the technology and missiles to launch a preemptive attack against the United States. The result was panic. In November, after the Russians launched another *Sputnik* with a dog aboard, Eisenhower's Gallup Poll rating plummeted. For the first time, the Democrats had a potent issue to use against the President: Where had Eisenhower been while the Russians were vaulting into first place? On the golf course? Senate Majority Leader Lyndon Johnson, who was usually on excellent terms with the President, complained, "It is not very reassuring to be told that next year, we will put a better satellite in the air. Perhaps it will even have chrome trim—and automatic windshield wipers."

Later that month, Eisenhower suffered a stroke. Nixon and Foster Dulles blamed the malady in part on the unprecedented criticism rained on him after *Sputnik.* The stroke did little permanent damage, save for damaging his ability to pronounce certain words and phrases. Within three weeks, he was well enough to fly to a NATO meeting in Paris. But, always a worrier, Mamie told a friend, "I'm not so sure we're ever going to be able to live in Gettysburg." John Eisenhower later surmised that under a parliamentary system, his father might have announced his retirement, effective after the 1958 elections.

After the stroke, the President was under the increased tyranny of his doctors, a fact that was partially concealed from the public. Hagerty justifiably feared that if the press and Washington rumor mill learned that Eisenhower daily took ten minutes of oxygen and often slept with the aid of Seconal, they might question his ability to keep on top of his job. Only a decade had passed since Republican orators wondered aloud whether Franklin Roosevelt's secret illness had caused him to give away too much to the Russians at Yalta. Eisenhower bore his medical regime with dignity, understood why the public must be kept from being alarmed about his condition, but hated it when he felt as if

March 1957: Sailing on the U.S.S. *Canberra,* Eisenhower attends a summit in Bermuda with the new British Prime Minister, his wartime friend Harold Macmillan. Sherman Adams and James Hagerty climb down in front of him.

he were being treated like an invalid. The private journal of his doctor, Howard Snyder:

"Mamie was present when I took the President's blood pressure . . . and she made a wry face. The President remarked, 'If it was any lower than that, I would forget my swear words,' and then he laughed." (October 1958)

"The President was insistent that I tell him his blood pressure. He was concerned because the diastolic pressure was creeping up, and he cussed the doctors who had encouraged him to accept a second term." (December 1958)

"The President . . . opened up a conversation by stating that he would go ahead and have his prostate troubles taken care of were it not for the fact that it would have to be the subject of so much discussion in the press. He asked me questions with intent to learn whether a simple 'Al Gruenther operation' (transurethral prostatotomy), which would keep him in only a few days, would not be entirely satisfactory. He even suggested that he could have this done while on a cruiser on a so-called vacation trip. This, of course, because he felt that he could avoid the publicity of the operation." (March 1959)

"The President complained of a pain in his left chest. He said he took a nitroglycerin last night, which worried Mamie. . . . I tried to pin him down as to whether the nitroglycerin had helped the pain, which would indicate a heart situation, but the President said no. . . . The President had never apprised me before the examination this morning of his having pains in his left chest. . . . [H]e indicated that he had been having the pain for several days and had not mentioned it. This is typical of the President." (March 1959)

"The President's golf was reasonably good on the first nine, but the worst I had ever seen on the second nine. The President was so mad that on the 17th green when he made a bad explosion shot out of the trap and I yelled, 'Fine shot!,' he got so mad he yelled, 'Fine shot, hell, you son of a bitch,' and threw his wedge at me. The staff of the club wrapped itself around my shins and the heavy iron wedge missed me; otherwise, I would have had a fractured leg." (April 1959)

L ittle Rock, September 1957 *(opposite):* **Angry white Arkansans heckle black students escorted into Little Rock Central High School by bayonet-carrying troops of the 101st Airborne Division on Eisenhower's reluctant order.**

153

A fter the shocks of *Sputnik* **and the Gaither Report, such prominent Democrats and Republicans as John Kennedy and Nelson Rockefeller (elected New York Governor in 1958) accused the administration of tolerating a Missile Gap that would put the United States behind the Russians in military strength. Eisenhower knew from secret intelligence that America was actually far ahead of the Russians in missile development. But to keep from compromising covert sources such as the U-2 spy flights over Russia, he angrily refused to say in public why he knew the charges were false.**

# Hell on Wings

Another source of presidential ire was advertisements by defense manufacturers such as these *(opposite)*, which appeared in *Aviation Week* and *Business Week*. Eisenhower thought that they fueled the Cold War. Denouncing "selfish" businessmen, he sometimes hurled an offending magazine into the Oval Office fireplace. Dramatizing his responsibilities as custodian of the nation's defense, he examines the *Discoverer XIII* satellite and the nuclear submarine *Nautilus*.

"Before I took his blood pressure, he stated he would not be surprised if it were considerably elevated; that he had lost his temper with a woman during the morning. . . . I said to him . . . that if he exploded, it probably would be a good thing physiologically because it was much worse to contain his anger and carry its ill effects with him. . . . I asked Charles [a White House butler] if the President were satisfied with vegetable salt or whether he continued to demand regular salt at his meals. . . . I suggested that Charles remove the regular shaker of salt to learn whether the President insisted on having it with his meals. . . . When the tray was served without a shaker of regular salt, the President went into a rage. He called me on the telephone, and with much profanity wanted to know what the hell I was doing. . . . Mrs. Eisenhower this morning . . . said she thought the President was going to have a stroke as a result of his conversation with me. . . . The President said he had a good night, but took the usual capsules of Seconal between midnight and morning." (January 1960)

The President responded to the national hysteria after *Sputnik* by establishing NASA and accelerating America's missile program. Although the Soviet triumph caused Americans to question their education system, he resisted demands for massive federal aid on grounds that it would unbalance the budget and hasten federal domination of public schools. A year after *Sputnik,* he cheerlessly signed a billion-dollar National Defense Education Act, which authorized long-term, low-interest loans for college students and grants to improve the teaching of science, mathematics, and foreign languages.

In December 1957, a rocket intended to launch the first American satellite exploded on the launch pad. The *Washington Post* published a story on the top-secret findings of Eisenhower's Gaither Commission on civil defense, suggesting that the panel had found "an America exposed to an almost immediate threat from the missile-bristling Soviet Union." Politicians and pundits warned of a Missile Gap that would allow the Kremlin "to open an almost unchallenged superiority in the nuclear striking power that was once our superiority," as the columnists Stewart and Joseph Alsop wrote.

Eisenhower had been horrified since 1945 by the danger that the United States would have to spend "unconscionable sums" for defense into eternity. He warned that the high taxes and deficits required to maintain such expense would reduce productivity, fuel inflation, and drive the American system to bankruptcy and totalitarianism. He wrote a friend, "Any person who doesn't clearly understand that national security and national solvency are mutually dependent and that permanent maintenance of a crushing weight of military power would eventually produce dictatorship should not be entrusted with any kind of responsibility in our country." Disturbed by a military-industrial establishment and Cold War psychosis that grew by feeding on each other, he told aides, "God help the nation when it has a President who doesn't know as much about the military as I do."

With his experience in intelligence assessment that dated back to

World War II, the President scrutinized public and private sources to gauge the Soviet threat. This included photographs and other material from the secret black U-2 spy planes whose periodic flights across Soviet defense and industrial sites he had begun authorizing in July 1956. He concluded that the Soviets were considerably behind the United States in missiles but felt that he could not reveal the evidence to Congress or the public without betraying secret American intelligence sources, especially the U-2. Thus the attack against him went on. Agonized by his inability to defend himself with all the resources at his disposal, he privately castigated the "sanctimonious, hypocritical bastards" exploiting the "false issue" of the Missile Gap. Ann Whitman once asked him how he had acquired his "ability to ignore attacks." From his mother, he replied—the "happiest person" he had ever known, despite "some great discouragements."

In his finest hour as President, Eisenhower held his ground against almost unbearable political pressure for a grand increase in defense spending—from Democrats and Republicans, many of whom worried about further losses in Congress. Only the American people's confidence that the old Supreme Commander would not let them down on military matters saved him from grave political damage. Virtually no one else who might have been President in those years could have carried off a similar feat. The result of Eisenhower's courage was that inflation was kept to an annual average of roughly 1 percent. The trajectory of the American-Soviet arms competition was held down.

In one respite from his unhappy year of 1957, Eisenhower exults over a well-placed shot during golf with a Senate friend, the father of a future President, Prescott Bush of Connecticut *(at left of Eisenhower).*

Dangerous antagonists over Chinese offshore islands: Mao Tse-tung and Chiang Kai-shek.

September 1958 (opposite): Eisenhower at Newport, followed by Hagerty and Sherman Adams, shortly before Adams's resignation amid scandal. The same month, the President cooks at a friend's Rhode Island estate. At left is his confidant, doctor, and scold, General Howard Snyder.

The Soviets began speaking in public about shifting more and more resources from military spending to improve the living standard of the average Russian.

For the first time since the Cold War began, the scene for a genuine détente had been set. The President told the *New York Times* columnist Arthur Krock that what he wanted "most of all" before leaving office was to reach "some agreement with the Soviet Union which would begin to take us along the road to reducing the plateau of tension and bring about a reduction in this terrible burden of armaments."

First he dealt with what appeared to be a challenge in the Middle East. In April 1957, the pro-Western President of Lebanon, Camille Chamoun, had complained of pan-Arab agitation against his regime. Under the new Eisenhower Doctrine, which pledged economic and military aid to Arab states threatened by the Soviet Union, Eisenhower had ordered units of the Sixth Fleet, plus Marines, into the eastern Mediterranean and offered to send them to Beirut. A year later, faced with a similar request by Chamoun, Eisenhower refused, wondering "what possible future there would be if we intervened, except to remain indefinitely." His reluctance was underscored by the fact that Lebanon was not under threat by external armies, as the doctrine required. The President's self-restraint was vindicated when the fighting in Lebanon ebbed away without American involvement.

In August 1958, the People's Republic of China used shelling and a naval blockade to reduce Nationalist China's ability to resupply Quemoy and Matsu, two Nationalist-held offshore islands long in dispute. This was not Eisenhower's first crisis over the Formosa Straits. In January 1955, after the communist Chinese moved against the Nationalist-held Tachen Islands, he had concluded that it was time to "draw the line." He ordered evacuation from the Tachens but allowed Foster Dulles and himself to imply that nuclear weapons could not be ruled out in the defense of Chiang Kai-shek's government on Taiwan. He told reporters that he saw "no reason why they shouldn't be just used exactly as you would a bullet or anything else." This warning shocked many Americans and American allies, but it helped to deter Beijing from further aggression. Privately the President insisted that "the time might come when the U.S. might have to intervene with atomic weapons, but that should come only at the end, and we would have to advise our allies first."

In the Formosa Straits crisis of 1958, Eisenhower warned that if Quemoy seemed on the verge of being overwhelmed, he would do whatever was necessary. To the area he ordered what was called the "most powerful air-naval striking force" in American history; it was well known that the force included nuclear weapons. By letter Khrushchev complained that "in the U.S.A. there are still people who do not want to part with the policy of threats and atomic blackmail. . . ." But Eisenhower's warnings quelled the threat of full Chinese invasion. Both sides backed away from what the President called "a Gilbert and Sullivan war." (Andrei Gromyko, the Soviet Foreign Minister, later

After Khrushchev's ultimatum on Berlin, Eisenhower cautions the American people not to overreact.

Fidel Castro after his New Year's 1959 revolution in Cuba.

recalled that during the crisis, Mao Tse-tung "flabbergasted" him by saying that in the event of war, Russia should allow the United States to penetrate deep into Chinese territory: "Only when the Americans are right in the central provinces should you give them everything you've got.")

On the eve of the 1958 congressional elections, Sherman Adams was accused of influence peddling on behalf of a New England textile man named Bernard Goldfine in exchange for gifts, including a soon-notorious vicuna coat. In mid-September, the President's doctor noted that public howls for Adams's ouster had caused Eisenhower to "have worked himself into a tense state." Around this time, the President told a friend with only some exaggeration that 1958 was fast becoming the "worst" year of his life. Suffering from Adams's resignation and an economic downturn dubbed the "Eisenhower recession," Republicans lost twelve seats in the Senate and forty-eight seats in the House.

That same month, Khrushchev resumed the pressure against West Berlin that Stalin had begun a decade before with the Berlin Blockade. He demanded that the Western powers agree on a German peace treaty within six months or face the prospect of losing access to their sector of the city. Having recently ousted Premier Bulganin to take full supreme power, Khrushchev privately reasoned that if he lacked the strategic strength to push the West to the bargaining table, he would do it by threatening one of its most vulnerable protectorates. Eisenhower told his son that if the West had to crash an East German blockade, the showdown could escalate to nuclear war: "In this gamble, we are not going to be betting white chips, building up gradually and gradually. Khrushchev should know that when we decide to act, our whole stack will be in the pot." Knowing that he might be "risking the very fate of civilization," the President met Khrushchev's bluff. He reinforced American troops in Europe to show that seizure of Europe would not be so easy and planned a new Berlin airlift, if necessary.

Congressmen demanded mobilization of American armed forces and a new surge in defense spending. Eisenhower kept his cool, assuming that one purpose of "Khrushchev's manufactured crisis" was to "frighten free populations and governments into unnecessary and debilitating spending sprees." With his skill in defusing confrontation, he calmly proceeded with a scheduled cut of thirty thousand men from the U. S. Army. As if to signal his intent not to let the Berlin crisis grow into war, Khrushchev in January 1959 sent one of his Deputy Premiers, Anastas Mikoyan, to Washington. In the Oval Office, Eisenhower told Mikoyan that he was prepared to use his final two years to "promote a better relationship" with the Soviet Union. The Berlin-Germany problem was remanded to the foreign ministers of the United States, Soviet Union, Britain, and France for negotiation at Geneva, where they were soon stalemated.

After the February 1959 resignation of Secretary of State Dulles, dying of cancer, Eisenhower appointed Under Secretary of State Christian Herter, an arthritis victim, to succeed him. As he and Herter wait to greet a foreign visitor at National Airport, the President shakes hands with Senate Majority Leader Lyndon Johnson. Eisenhower valued the cooperation he received from Johnson and House Speaker Sam Rayburn but was not always comfortable with Johnson's intense manner. Once when the Texas Senator came to the Oval Office, Eisenhower stationed an aide between them to keep Johnson from seizing him around the shoulder. He had told the aide his bursitis was "acting up."

161

In June Khrushchev sent another Deputy Premier, Frol Kozlov, to open a Soviet art and technology exhibition in New York. At the White House, Kozlov suggested that the President meet Khrushchev at a summit: "Why should our two countries fight each other? If we take the Berlin problem, it should be resolved by the Germans themselves. After all, it was they who twice imposed war on us, so why should we fight because of them?" Three months before this hint, Eisenhower had already agreed with Harold Macmillan, British Prime Minister, to ask for such a meeting once progress on Berlin had been made at Geneva. Now the President asked his wartime colleague Robert Murphy of the State Department to inform Kozlov that if there was progress in Geneva, the President and Khrushchev could hold informal talks in the United States.

By error, Murphy gave Kozlov the invitation unconditionally. Khrushchev immediately accepted. Furious, the President told aides he must now "pay the penalty" of a meeting that, in light of the Geneva stalemate, would be "a most unpleasant experience." Nonetheless he wrote Khrushchev, "I have no other purpose than to help bring about agreements in which we can have mutual confidence, designed to promote better understandings, greater tolerance, and peaceful development among the world's peoples including the U.S.S.R. and the U.S."

In mid-September, Khrushchev's silver plane landed at Andrews Air Force Base for the first American visit of a supreme Soviet leader. Khrushchev later recalled that it "shook me up a bit. Here was the United States of America . . . bestowing honor on the representative of our socialist homeland—a country which, in the eyes of capitalist America, had always been unworthy or, worse, infected with some

Khrushchev in America, September 1959: Posing with Eisenhower and Nixon in the Oval Office *(above),* the Soviet Premier infuriates the President by boastfully handing him a Soviet space trophy. Eisenhower presumes that Khrushchev's purpose is to twit him with a reminder of Soviet superiority in space. In Hollywood *(below),* Khrushchev visits the set of *Can-Can.* At Camp David *(opposite),* he and Eisenhower pause before entering the presidential lodge, Aspen.

163

The President tours the world, November–December 1959. He reads briefing materials aboard *Air Force One,* the first presidential jet plane, brought into service two months earlier. In Paris, he meets with British Prime Minister Harold Macmillan, French President Charles de Gaulle, West German Chancellor Konrad Adenauer, and French Premier Michel Debré. Opposite, below, is a motorcade in Turkey. In Iran *(top),* Eisenhower is welcomed by the Shah, who knows that he owes the President his throne. In India *(middle),* he finds it difficult to deal with what he considers the moral abstractions of Prime Minister Jawaharlal Nehru, here at the Taj Mahal, but six million Indians *(bottom)* turn out for the most populous greeting of Eisenhower's life.

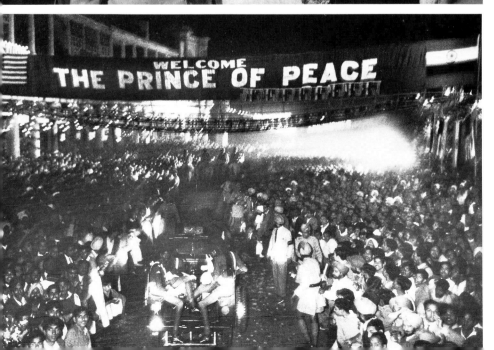

BRAZILIAN INDUSTRY
JOINS WITH ALL THE PEOPLE OF BRAZIL IN SAYING
WELCOME IKE
SESI E FED. DAS INDÚSTRIAS DO D. FEDERAL

sort of plague." After a week-long tour of Washington, New York, Los Angeles, San Francisco, Des Moines, and Pittsburgh, the two most powerful men on earth retired with their closest aides for a weekend at the Maryland presidential retreat Eisenhower had renamed after his grandson, Camp David.

The President noted that when he and Khrushchev were alone, "he was very convivial with me, especially eager to be friendly," but when Gromyko and other Russians appeared, he "kept reminding me that he would have to take up these matters with his government." By Sunday afternoon, Khrushchev had lifted his Berlin ultimatum; Eisenhower had agreed to serious negotiations, a full-scale four-power summit meeting and a return trip to the Soviet Union in 1960. Before leaving, Khrushchev told reporters, "I would like to wish that we more and more frequently use in the relations between our two countries that short and good American word—*Okay!*"

That winter, the President demonstrated how many nations saw the United States and its leaders as something other than wicked imperialists, saying, "Such prestige and standing as I have on the earth, I want to use it." In December, he boarded the new presidential jet, *Air Force One*, for a three-week goodwill journey to Rome, Ankara, Karachi, Kabul, Tehran, and New Delhi, where six million cried, "Long live the King of America!" Then on to Athens, Tunis, Paris, Madrid, Casablanca. Two months later, he made a similar trip through South America that consolidated his standing as the leader whom the world most respected and loved. In mid-May, he would go to the summit with Khrushchev, Macmillan, and Charles de Gaulle, now the new French President, in Paris. In June, he would fly to Moscow for the first state tour of the Soviet Union by an American President.

In Geneva, negotiators were drawing near to agreement on a nuclear test ban that, if signed, would be the first major accord of the Cold War. Eisenhower told aides that he was "determined" to reach it, perhaps at the Paris summit. He told Macmillan that such a treaty would be "a ray of light in a world that is bound to be weary of the tensions brought about by mutual suspicion, distrust and arms races." On the heels of agreement, he hoped that the American presidential candidates of 1960 would compete largely on the basis of who could best expand his opening to the Russians. He told de Gaulle, "What a splendid exit it would be for me to end up . . . with an agreement between East and West."

That spring, the CIA pressed him for more U-2 flights over the Soviet Union. The Agency was looking most of all for operational Soviet intercontinental ballistic missiles, and had yet to find one. New intelligence suggested that such ICBMs might be standing at Plesetsk. After nearly four years of flights, Eisenhower was worried that the Soviets might have gained the capacity to down one of the planes. He worried about the effect on the new dialogue with Khrushchev. He had warned aides in February 1960 that "if one of these aircraft were lost when we were engaged in apparently sincere deliberations, it could

In February 1960, the President flies to Latin America. Here he is shown with a Brazilian senate leader, Evandro Mendez Viana, in Rio de Janeiro.

On May Day, 1960, a CIA U-2 spy plane flown by Francis Gary Powers (shown here during his Moscow trial) crashes deep in the Soviet Union, starting an escalation between Washington and Moscow that culminates in the wrecking of the Paris summit and Eisenhower's hopes for relieving the Cold War. Leaving the Elysée Palace *(below)*, a disappointed Macmillan and Eisenhower are briefed by General Andrew Goodpaster. On Eisenhower's return from Paris *(opposite, above)*, citizens of Washington stage a consoling welcome on Pennsylvania Avenue. In September, when Khrushchev arrives at the United Nations *(opposite, below)*, picketers demonstrate the frigid new Cold War atmosphere in the United States.

be put on display in Moscow and ruin my effectiveness." He agreed to more flights, but not during the fortnight before the summit.

On Sunday, May 1, the final day before the President's ban, the CIA's Francis Gary Powers flew one of the black planes from Peshawar, Pakistan, for a thirteen-hour flight over the Soviet Union to Norway. Shooting skeet that afternoon at Camp David, Eisenhower was called to the telephone and told by his staff secretary and close aide, General Andrew Goodpaster, that the plane was "possibly lost." At the White House the next morning, assured by the CIA that no pilot could survive a U-2 downing, the President privately approved issuance of a NASA cover story claiming that one of its "research" planes had evidently strayed across the Soviet border from Turkey and was lost.

Three days later, Khrushchev announced the downing of an "aggressive" American plane on May Day. NASA responded with a further elaboration of its cover story. Then Khrushchev announced, "We have the remnants of the plane—and we also have the pilot, who is quite alive and kicking!" Until now the deceptions issued by the American government had not come from Eisenhower's lips. Some around him suggested that he announce that the U-2 flight had been made without his orders. This would preserve the summit but it would allow Khrushchev to trap the President himself in a lie. It would also give credence to the years of complaints that Eisenhower was not on top of his job: Was the President so inattentive that without his knowledge the CIA could send a pilot into the Soviet Union and perhaps provoke nuclear war?

Eisenhower took responsibility for the incursion but refused to apologize for it to Khrushchev. The four years of flights, he maintained, were compelled by Soviet secrecy. With his father in Paris on Sunday, May 14, the day before the summit was to begin, John Eisenhower recorded Khrushchev's demand that "the United States renounce the act of sending spying planes over Russia, renounce any intention of doing so in the future and punish those responsible. . . . The President decided this is not time to be bulldozed." The four-

power meeting at the Elysée Palace turned from dream to nightmare. When Eisenhower met only the second of Khrushchev's three conditions, the Soviet leader stormed out, insisting that he would not negotiate with the United States until it elected a new leader in November. The President's trip to Russia was cancelled. The Soviets broke off the test ban talks in Geneva.

That summer, Snyder noticed that the President had "lost his sparkle. His facial expressions at most times seem grim and determined." His "empire of glory" seemed to be "crumbling about his head." Eisenhower told his science advisor, George Kistiakowsky, that in recent years he had concentrated his efforts on ending the Cold War and felt that he had been making "big progress." Then the "stupid U-2 mess" came and ruined all of his efforts. Now there was "nothing worthwhile" left to do before the end of his term.

Before the July party conventions, the President privately told Arthur Krock that he couldn't comprehend how the Democrats could consider choosing such an "inexperienced boy" as Senator John Kennedy of Massachusetts—or for that matter, Stevenson or Senator Stuart Symington of Missouri, one of Eisenhower's chief antagonists on the Missile Gap. He said, "Lyndon Johnson has retreated some from sound positions for partisan causes, but he would be the best Democrat of them all as President from the viewpoint of responsible management of the national interest." As for his own party, the President said he had never met with a man "with whose mind my mind clicks" as constantly as it did with Nixon's. The Vice President's main rival was Governor Nelson Rockefeller of New York, a first-term member of the Eisenhower sub-Cabinet who had run afoul of the President on the Missile Gap. Eisenhower said that Rockefeller was "a well-meaning fellow" but "madly ambitious . . . obsessed with studies and blueprints and polls."

Krock noted in his journal, "He was in great good humor and talked very calmly of his problems. But he said he often wakens in the night 'and then, oh boy!' I advised him to have a bedside tape recorder so that his speeches would sound more like the easy way he expresses himself, hanging participles and all. But he said he can't 'talk into those

170

In 1960, the CIA pursued assassination plots against Patrice Lumumba of the Congo and Fidel Castro, the latter shown here with Khrushchev during their fall visit to the United Nations. Eisenhower's knowledge of these plots has never been established. Fifteen years later, when the U.S. Senate investigated them, along with others under later administrations, John Eisenhower defended his father by recalling his view that "no man is indispensable."

things.' And as for his news conference syntax, he said, 'What the hell if I leave out verbs, hitch singular nouns to plural verbs and all that? They know what I mean, and that's what's important.' "

That month, Eisenhower faced possible mutiny in his own party. Citing the Paris debacle, Rockefeller demanded $3 billion more per year in defense spending, deplored the Missile Gap, announced that he would accept a convention draft for President, and threatened a floor fight against a platform rubber-stamping the Eisenhower policies. To remove the danger, Nixon vainly asked the Governor to run with him for Vice President. Then the two men crafted a joint statement implying that Nixon had endorsed key elements of Rockefeller's critique. The President called Nixon and icily said that it would be "difficult" for him to support a platform which showed no "respect for the record of the Republican Administration." New language was found to satisfy all sides, but the episode added a new reservation to Eisenhower's complex feelings about his Vice President.

Whatever ambivalence he felt toward Nixon was mitigated by his disdain for the Democratic presidential nominee, whom he privately called "Little Boy Blue." He felt that money, public relations, and political manipulation had allowed a man who was too young and inexperienced to grab the Democratic nomination. Appalled, he listened to his friend Ellis "Slats" Slater, who had known Joseph Kennedy as a fellow liquor mogul and warned that the Kennedys intended to build a political dynasty "like Tammany Hall" that would control the White House for years to come. By now, Eisenhower was feeling little more friendly toward Lyndon Johnson, the Democratic vice presidential nominee. Around close friends he recalled Johnson warning him that Jack Kennedy was a "dangerous man": "The next thing I knew, I turned on television and there was that son of a bitch becoming a Vice Presidential candidate with this 'dangerous man.' Haven't talked to him since."

At an August press conference, the President accidentally shot Nixon in the foot. Citing the Vice President's campaign slogan, "It's Experience That Counts," a reporter asked for an example of a major idea of Nixon's that he had adopted. Eisenhower replied, "If you give me a week, I'll think of one. I don't remember." The answer was informed by his natural indignation about any suggestion that anyone but he made his government's decisions. Nonetheless Democrats seized the comment to deflate Nixon's claims of experience at the President's side. It was widely read as a signal of Eisenhower's indifference toward Nixon's election. And it hurt.

The President's chagrin at his gaffe only increased his will to help defeat Kennedy. He felt so strongly that it marred his health. In mid-October, as Eisenhower campaigned for Nixon, Dr. Snyder recorded that his patient suffered a "bizarre cardiac reaction" to a United Auto Workers leaflet saying that a vote for Nixon was a vote for bigotry: "When he received the Key to the City of Detroit . . . his lips were so tight that he could hardly smile." Later that month, Snyder noted that

Eisenhower's private first choice to succeed him in 1961 was his Secretary of the Treasury, Robert B. Anderson, a onetime Democratic member of the Texas legislature—"just about the ablest man I know anywhere," he wrote Swede Hazlett. In 1956, when Eisenhower prodded Anderson to think of the Vice Presidency, the Texan bluntly replied, "You say you know a lot of people who would back me. But can you tell me that a lifelong Republican in Kansas would? He'd ask, 'How long has this guy been a Republican? He's just walking in and asking for the nomination.' " Undeterred, Eisenhower privately said in 1957, "Of all these fellows, the one who has the broadest gauge—best in experience and sense and the right age—it's that Bob Anderson. Boy, I'd like to fight for him in 1960!" As the 1960 election approached, he told Anderson, "I'll quit what I'm doing, Bob, I'll raise money, I'll make speeches. I'll do *anything* to help. Just tell me I'm at liberty." But Anderson refused, concluding that he did not have the drive to seek the Presidency and that without it, he could not hope to win.

After the Republicans nominate Nixon and Lodge in Chicago, Eisenhower receives the two men *(below)* at his summer vacation quarters in Newport, Rhode Island. Once the three men are inside *(above)*, the President shows his continuing irritation at Nixon's effort to win Nelson Rockefeller's support by momentarily aligning himself with Rockefeller's criticisms of the administration. Nixon's eagerness to mollify the President was one reason for choosing Lodge, who was Eisenhower's first choice for Vice President.

after "a prolonged conference on political techniques with Vice President Nixon and his group of advisors," the President was "very fatigued." The doctor asked him to take more daily oxygen to keep up with the pace.

Snyder wrote in his diary: "Mamie was plugging at me to tell the President he had to quit speaking and working for Nixon—that he might pop a cork. I have been cautioning him in this regard during the past several weeks since he became involved in a direct effort to elect Nixon." On November 1, the doctor told Nixon that he could not approve the President's planned heavy campaign schedule. Kennedy's attacks had raised his "dander"; the strain of intense campaigning might be too much for his limited cardiac reserves. Snyder said to Mamie Eisenhower, "I know what he *wants* to do, and he usually won't take my advice. Please, either talk him out of it or just don't let him do it—for the sake of his health." A distraught Mamie sent an S.O.S. to Pat Nixon, cautioning her that "Ike must never know I called you."

That afternoon, Nixon came to the White House and noted that he had "rarely seen Eisenhower more animated." Soon the President was to leave for downstate Illinois, upstate New York, and Michigan, where the race was especially close. "He was confused, to put it mildly, when I opened the discussion with half a dozen rather lame reasons for his not carrying out the expanded itinerary. At first he was hurt and

August 1960: At a press conference, Eisenhower unwittingly deals a harmful blow to Nixon's candidacy. Asked about a major idea of Nixon's that he had adopted, the President replies, "If you give me a week, I might think of one."

October 1960: Eisenhower campaigns for Nixon in New York City (with New York Republican Senators Kenneth Keating and Jacob Javits at right) and sits with Pat Nixon on a platform. The journalist Theodore White, watching from the crowd, wrote that "Eisenhower has, and retains, a magic in American politics that is peculiarly his: he makes people happy." Later, after Nixon asked the President to leave the campaign to spare his health, an angry Eisenhower told his aides, "Damn it, he looks like a loser to me."

The presidential contenders, fall 1960 *(right)*.

then he was angry. . . . His pride prevented him from saying anything, but I knew that he was puzzled and frustrated by my conduct." Nixon's request of Eisenhower to stop campaigning very likely cost him the Presidency.

On election night, the President did not stay up to hear the results. Learning the next morning of Nixon's apparent defeat, he told Mamie that only one other time had he felt that life was not worth living—at West Point, when he was told that his injured knee would keep him from ever playing football again. Wondering whether he could have turned the tide by making the extra campaign speeches, he called the election a "repudiation," the "biggest defeat of my life": "All I've been trying to do for eight years has gone down the drain. I might just as well have been having fun." He felt as if he had been "hit in the solar plexus with a ball bat."

Flying to Augusta, Georgia, for a postelection rest, he complained, "Dick never asked me how I thought the campaign should be run." He had offered Nixon the services of his television consultant, the actor Robert Montgomery, "who would never have let him look as he did in that first television debate. Cabot Lodge should never have stuck his nose into the makeup of the Cabinet. Promising a Negro cost us thousands of votes in the South, maybe South Carolina and Texas."

Winter came. The Kennedy inaugural reviewing stand went up in front of the White House. Eisenhower said to friends, "It's like being in the death cell and watching them put up the scaffold." As the press pronounced itself dazzled by the qualities of the incoming President, the retiring one told a friend, "We have a new genius in our midst who is incapable of making any mistakes and therefore deserving of no criticism whatsoever." Poignantly he wondered, "What happened to all those fine young people with stars in their eyes who sailed balloons and rang doorbells for us in 1952?"

The President privately worried about Kennedy's campaign pledge to cut taxes and increase the defense budget by deficit spending, if necessary: "I'm going to insist on a balanced budget, no matter what Kennedy says he wants." When Eisenhower's Under Secretary of State, the Republican financier Douglas Dillon, agreed to become Kennedy's Treasury Secretary, the outgoing President was irate at the notion that it might suggest his own approval of Kennedy's fiscal policies. But when the President-elect came to see him and his aides in early December, Eisenhower behaved with dignity, pronouncing himself impressed by Kennedy's "warmth and modesty." One wonders whether, with his constant memories of his lost first son, he ever mused upon the fact that had Icky lived, he would have been exactly the same age as the new President.

In this and another White House meeting the day before Kennedy's swearing-in, Eisenhower was genuinely impressed by his successor's good manners and intelligence as a "serious, earnest seeker for information," but feared that the President-elect seemed to think he could run the Executive Branch the same way he had run his Senate office.

Election eve, November 1960: Before midnight, Eisenhower views Nixon on a television monitor during a national campaign broadcast on which he has just appeared.

He noted that Kennedy "looked upon the Presidency as not only a very personal thing, but as an institution that one man could handle with an individual assistant here and another there," and that he "had no idea of the complexity of the job."

Since Fidel Castro's New Year's 1959 revolution in Cuba, hope that the new regime might be drawn into friendship with the United States had turned into anxiety that Cuba was drifting into the Soviet orbit. By December 1960, the CIA was training a paramilitary brigade of Cuban exiles in Guatemala for a counterrevolutionary invasion; it also halfheartedly pursued schemes to assassinate Castro. (As with similar operations against Patrice Lumumba in the Congo and other foreign leaders in the 1950s, there is no conclusive evidence that Eisenhower knew of the death plots.) The President told his Director of Central Intelligence, Allen Dulles, that he would approve no invasion of Cuba at least until there was a genuine government-in-exile. In early January 1961, Eisenhower broke diplomatic relations with Castro.

Three days before Kennedy's inauguration, Eisenhower went to the Oval Office to deliver a Farewell Address to the American people, just as his hero George Washington had. In a conspicuous warning to his successor, he said, "We cannot mortgage the material assets of our grandchildren without risking the loss also of their political and spiritual heritage." He wished he could report "that a lasting peace is in sight," but could say only that for eight years "war has been avoided." Returning full circle to the theme of his Chance for Peace address in the spring of 1953, he expressed his deepest convictions with a long-remembered warning against "the acquisition of unwarranted influence, whether sought or unsought, by the military-industrial complex."

Some who had no idea of the energy Eisenhower had spent during his second term to resist demands for more military spending to escalate the Cold War thought this an eccentric utterance by a President whom they had seen as a front man for the Pentagon and Big Business. In fact, an early draft of the speech lambasted the danger of a mutually reinforcing "military-industrial-*Congressional* complex," but Eisenhower took out the third leg of the triangle in order not to throw a final brickbat over his shoulder at Congress. At a press conference the morning after the speech, he warned against the "insidious penetration of our own minds that the only thing this country is engaged in is weaponry and missiles. And I'll tell you we just can't afford to do that."

On Friday morning, January 20, 1961, as Washington recovered from an inaugural eve blizzard, John Eisenhower found the atmosphere around the Oval Office "eerie": "Dad spent a good deal of the morning leaning on his safe talking with Ann Whitman and others." After the Kennedys arrived, Mamie said, "Look at Ike in his top hat. He looks just like Paddy the Irishman." Leaving for the Capitol, John "choked up a bit. Our direct connection with the magnificent White House was over."

With public courtesy and private doubts, Eisenhower receives President-elect Kennedy at the White House, December 1960 and January 1961. Christian Herter and Robert Anderson (at edge of picture) flank the two leaders.

January 17, 1961, in the Oval Office before the President gave his Farewell Address: "We must guard against the acquisition of unwarranted influence, whether sought or unsought, by the military-industrial complex." Liberals delighted to hear these words did not know that they conveyed one of his most profound anxieties.

As Kennedy spoke with Eisenhower during their drive up Pennsylvania Avenue and on the inaugural platform, he was courtesy itself. Privately he lamented the necessity of taking power in the shadow of the best-loved President of the century. Robert Kennedy later recalled that on inaugural morning, when his brother mentioned Cornelius Ryan's bestseller about D-Day, *The Longest Day,* "he was fascinated that Eisenhower had never read the book—and in fact hadn't seemed to have read anything! . . . He thought he had a rather fascinating personality and could understand, talking to him, why he was President of the United States. . . . I think he just felt that he hadn't done his homework, and he didn't know a good deal about areas that he should know. I think he always felt that Eisenhower was unhappy with him—that he was so young and elected President."

After the ceremony, Richard Nixon and other high-ranking Eisenhower alumni, many faces glowing with tears, fêted the former President at the F Street Club. Eisenhower later said that he and Mamie then made the "fantastic discovery" that "we were free—as only private citizens in a democratic nation can be free." They were driven eighty miles through the deep snow to Pennsylvania. There after nightfall, for the first time in years, Eisenhower hopped out of his car and opened the gate himself: "And so we came to Gettysburg and to the farm we had bought eleven years earlier, where we expected to spend the remainder of our lives."

January 19, 1961: On the day before he leaves office, Eisenhower invites Nixon to the Oval Office for a last conversation and awards citations to members of his inner circle *(below)*. At left are Christian Herter and Thomas Gates, his third and last Secretary of Defense. Facing Eisenhower is General Goodpaster. At right, reading the citations aloud, is John Eisenhower.

Friday, January 20, 1961: On Eisenhower's final morning as President, his secretary, Ann Whitman, knots his formal tie for the inaugural ceremonies *(opposite, above).*

In the Red Room, he and the President-elect wait uneasily, along with Senator John Sparkman of Alabama *(left),* Jacqueline Kennedy, and Speaker of the House Sam Rayburn *(right),* before they drive to the Capitol.

No longer President, Eisenhower speaks to Chet Huntley of NBC before he and Mamie depart an emotional luncheon with outgoing staff and Cabinet members for the eighty-mile drive to Gettysburg. (Behind them are the John Eisenhowers and the Richard Nixons.)

The following Monday, having shed the cares of office, Eisenhower shoots at a friend's plantation in Albany, Georgia.

# 6.
# "REMAINDER OF
# OUR LIVES"

Even for a former President with as healthy a psyche as Eisenhower's, sudden decompression after twenty years of great power was not painless. Dr. Snyder recorded that the weekend after the Eisenhowers returned to Gettysburg, "he and Mamie were snowbound in the house. There was considerable friction between them during these days, and I am sure the President was very happy to get away. . . . " Eisenhower flew to the Georgia plantation of his friend W. Alton "Pete" Jones, president of Cities Service Oil, on Jones's private plane. Snyder wrote, "Within fifteen minutes, the President had changed into shooting clothes and we were out after quail. . . . Pete and the President each bagged the limit." In Washington, a special act of Congress restored Eisenhower's rank as General of the Army.

In February, owing to Mamie's aversion to flying, the couple took the train to Palm Desert, California, where they thenceforth spent each winter. By April, they were back in Gettysburg, where it was planting time. While Eisenhower was at Columbia, he and Mamie had looked for the permanent home they had never had during the decades in the Army. His Pennsylvania Dutch ancestors had lived on a farm fifty miles from Gettysburg; he knew the town well from his assignment to Camp Colt during World War I. In 1950, they bought the rich acreage on the edge of the Civil War battlefield. Friends bought adjoining parcels of land to ensure privacy. The old red farmhouse, once used by Confederate troops, was largely dismantled and reconstructed as the heart of a new white edifice with a glassed-in sunporch. Completed in 1955 for the President's retirement, the house instead had its first extended occupancy during Eisenhower's convalescence from the heart attack.

The General resigned himself to the as-

The farm at Gettysburg: From the air (opposite) and as interpreted by Grandma Moses.

sumption that "this kind of farm can never make money." His main interest was in leaving "a heritage of improved farmland in Gettysburg by means of a planned feed production program in which the manure will be returned to the soil to enrich impoverished areas." He rotated crops and pastures, raising hay, corn, oats, barley, soybeans, sorghum. Of his roughly one hundred prize Angus cattle he butchered more than he sold, loathe to risk inferior livestock that might be publicly known as "Eisenhower Angus." John and Barbara Eisenhower and their children lived a mile away in a converted schoolhouse to which John had moved his family from Washington pressures and publicity during his father's second term.

In April 1961, the CIA's tiny paramilitary force landed in Cuba. Lacking air cover or reinforcements, the Cuban exiles were killed or captured at the Bay of Pigs, hurling President Kennedy and his government into their first crisis. In Gettysburg, Eisenhower mentioned to his son that an Iowa woman had wired him: "You go down there and tell that little boy to be careful. In fact, you'd better go and take over yourself."

Largely to prevent Eisenhower from issuing damaging public criticism of the affair, Kennedy asked him to Camp David and described what had happened. Like a schoolmaster dressing down a child, Eisenhower asked him (according to his notes), "Mr. President, before you approved this plan did you have everybody in front of you debating the thing so you got pros and cons yourself and then made your decision, or did you see these people one of a time?" Kennedy told him, "No one knows how tough this job is until after he has been in it a few months." Eisenhower: "If you will forgive me, I think I mentioned that to you three months ago." Kennedy: "I assure you that hereafter, if we get in anything like this, it is going to be a success." Eisenhower: "Well, I am glad to hear that."

Publicly the President took full responsibility, but Eisenhower was furious when some Kennedy officials, ignoring the difference between building a resource and using it, insisted to newsmen off the record that the Bay of Pigs was actually Eisenhower's fault. The General told friends that the fiasco "could not have happened in my Administration." John jokingly urged him to issue a statement saying, "I don't run no bad invasions." (Eisenhower refused, calling the idea "small-minded.") Informed about further details of the operation, the General wrote in his diary that "this story could be called a 'Profile in Timidity and Indecision.' "

Eisenhower's friend Ellis Slater found him "terribly unhappy" about what he saw as Kennedy's "careless spending" and indifference to inflation, not to mention "the continuing buildup of the military, the space scientists and the armament industries. This combination can be so powerful and the military machine so big it just has to be used." In May, when Kennedy committed the United States to an expensive moon landing by 1970, partly to renew American prestige after the Bay of Pigs, Eisenhower was even more unhappy. He later wrote one of the astronauts that the "unwise" moon challenge had disrupted a "thoughtfully planned" space program by granting highest priority "to a race, in other words, a stunt."

In August, when the Berlin Wall was built, Eisenhower noted that the Potsdam agreement allowed the four victors of World War II "the absolute right to use whatever force was needed to eliminate walls" between the sectors of the city. He said that were he in charge, the Wall would have been knocked down. More willing to consider use of force in retirement than when in power, he was disgusted that the President did not agree.

When Eisenhower learned that the Kennedys had used Mount Vernon, the sacred preserve of his hero, for a sparkling evening of dinner and dancing in honor of the President of Pakistan, one of his aides

The farmer worries about his cattle.

John Eisenhower wrote that after the return to Gettysburg, "I was shocked and worried at the Old Man's demeanor. His movements were slower, his tone less sharp, and he had time even during the work day to stop and indulge in what would formerly be considered casual conversation. I feared for his health." John finally concluded that his father had "simply relaxed." Nevertheless Eisenhower had to adjust to a schedule with fewer demands than at any time since the Philippines in the late 1930s. These 1961 photographs show a man whose sagging face and posture are very different from the upright, electric figure of the war and Presidency. Sitting with the former President is his secretary since 1952, Ann Whitman, who endured her own severe letdown. She finally left Eisenhower's employ to work for Nelson Rockefeller.

While planning his presidential library, Eisenhower flew in November 1961 to Independence, Missouri, where Harry Truman showed him through his own archive. As this photograph reveals, their nine-year-old animosity was not ended.

March 1962: President Kennedy calls on his predecessor in Palm Desert, California.

found him "the angriest I ever saw him," crying, "What a desecration! These goddamn—" He leaned back and grinned: "The doctors say I shouldn't get my blood pressure up, so I guess I shouldn't say any more." On another occasion: "You can always tell a Harvard man, but you can't tell him much." He privately referred to his successor as "the Boy."

When Allen Dulles resigned from the CIA five months after the Bay of Pigs, Kennedy replaced him with John McCone, who had chaired Eisenhower's Atomic Energy Commission. Kennedy asked McCone to brief his old boss from time to time and try to keep him on the reservation. It did little good. Robert Kennedy recalled how McCone reported that "Eisenhower would be getting madder and madder. . . . He was the one influence with Eisenhower which was giving him another side and moderating what Eisenhower was hearing all the time. He used to say to me that Eisenhower would sit out there —he was not informed—and he'd just be filled with poison by all of these people who would tell him things and make things up."

On May Day, 1962, the hundredth anniversary of Ida Eisenhower's birth, the General and Mamie went to Abilene to dedicate the Dwight D. Eisenhower Library, built on a section of rich, black soil where he had planted sweet corn as a boy. Kennedy did not attend but sent Lyndon Johnson, whose helicopter landed noisily during the ceremonies. The General told the crowd of twenty-five thousand—the largest in Abilene's history, larger than his homecomings in 1945 and 1952— that Ida's sons "would like today to think that she knows that they still revere her teaching, her strength, her refusal ever to admit defeat in small or great things."

Eisenhower's speech reflected his sense of alienation from Kennedy's America: "We venerate the pioneers who fought droughts and

floods, isolation and Indians, to come to Kansas and westward. . . . Now I wonder if some of those people could come back today and see us doing the twist instead of the minuet. . . . When we see movies and the stage and books and periodicals using vulgarity, sensuality, indeed, downright filth to sell their wares . . . do you say America has advanced as much as we have materially? When we see our very art forms so changed that the works of Michelangelo and Leonardo da Vinci are scarcely spoken of in terms of a piece of canvas that looks like a broken down tin lizzie loaded with paint has been driven over it? What has happened to our concept of beauty and decency and morality?"

Eisenhower maintained the ambition to make the Republicans a moderate, majority party that he had failed to achieve while President. Throughout his two terms, he had toyed with the term "Americans for Modern Republicanism," once jotting on a notepad the initials "A.M.R." Party regulars had been dismayed when he turned over portions of his 1952 and 1956 campaigns to independent "citizens" groups. Occasionally he daydreamed about starting a centrist third party. In 1962, appointed honorary chairman of a group called the Republican Citizens, he said, "What we're trying to do is build a bridge between the Republican Party on the one hand and the Independents and dissatisfied Democrats on the other so that these latter people may eventually find themselves more comfortable living with Republican policies and personalities."

During the 1962 midterm campaign, Eisenhower made twenty-eight speeches for candidates in twenty-one states and starred at more than two dozen fundraising dinners. Kennedy blamed the General's seemingly newfound eagerness for partisan campaigning on a poll asking seventy-five historians and political scientists to rank American Presidents in order of greatness. Taken earlier that year by the Harvard historian Arthur Schlesinger, Sr., the survey found Eisenhower twenty-second, at the bottom of the "average" category, along with Chester Arthur and Andrew Johnson. Kennedy told his aide, Arthur Schlesinger, Jr., "Eisenhower has been going along for years, basking in the glow of applause he has always had. Then he saw that poll and realized how he stood before the cold eye of history—way below Truman; even below Hoover. Now he's mad to save his reputation."

Eisenhower in 1962 was more scathing than he had ever dared to be while President. At times he sounded almost like Nixon in 1960: "I'm sick and tired of people telling the American people they did nothing for eight years." He attacked the "so-called brilliant" young men running down America—"callow youths . . . reckless men whose primary objective is political gain." He scoffed at the Kennedy administration's "sophisticated nonsense." He said that the "dreary foreign record of the past twenty-one months" was "too sad to talk about," and denounced the Senate campaign of Edward Kennedy (whom he privately called "the Bonus Baby") as "crass, almost arrogant."

193

"Ike and Dick" together again, fall 1962, during Nixon's campaign for Governor of California.

For a CBS program called "D-Day-plus-20," Eisenhower returns with Walter Cronkite in the summer of 1963 to the scene of his greatest triumph.

On October 20, McCone asked him to Washington, where he revealed that a U-2 spy plane had found offensive missiles in Cuba. After making his decision the next day to blockade the island, Kennedy won Eisenhower's endorsement with a telephone call to Gettysburg. A week later, he informed him by telephone of the tentative settlement with Khrushchev, which included an American promise not to invade Cuba and American inspection of the island's military sites. "Of course, it was never done," Eisenhower later complained. "And I think the communists probably concluded he wouldn't do anything. But I insisted on this land inspection. . . . It was an opportunity we missed not to go in." Like Suez and Hungary in 1956, the Cuban Missile Crisis rallied Americans around their President. Contrary to tradition, the party holding the White House gained seats in Congress. Richard Nixon blamed his loss of the California governorship largely on "the Cuban thing." The Republicans remained a minority. The Republican Citizens vanished.

Since World War II, Eisenhower had refused honoraria for speeches, believing that a former President should not serve on corporate boards. His income from *Crusade in Europe* had been well invested, and he could rely on military and presidential pensions. In early 1961, he agreed to write *The White House Years* in two volumes for Doubleday, with the help of his son John, William Ewald, one of his former speechwriters, and Samuel Vaughan, a young Doubleday editor. *Mandate for Change* was published in 1963, *Waging Peace* in 1965. Eisenhower's staff system was probably better for presidential management than for the writing of presidential memoirs. Though deservedly praised for their accuracy and comprehensiveness, the two volumes were far more defensive than *Crusade,* lacked the sound of Eisenhower's voice (as his old Abilene friend Ruby Norman noticed when she read them), and were neither commercial nor critical successes. Of the first volume Kennedy joked, "Apparently Ike never did anything wrong."

On the hundredth anniversary of Lincoln's Gettysburg Address, with Governor William Scranton of Pennsylvania, November 1963. Eisenhower would have been pleased to see Scranton elected President in 1964 but never openly endorsed him.

November 1963: At John Kennedy's funeral, Washington, D.C.

On Friday, November 22, 1963, Eisenhower was in New York for a UN luncheon when told the news from Dallas. He said, "There is bound to be a psychotic sort of accident sometime." Characteristically his first instinct was to think of how Americans might be kept from going into crisis. Thus he disapproved of the continuous assassination and funeral coverage on television: Cancelling commercials was a proper gesture of respect but an hourly five-minute news summary would have been "less disturbing" to the American people. On Saturday morning, Eisenhower's old on-and-off comrade Lyndon Johnson invited him to the White House and told him essentially what he told Adlai Stevenson, another leader whom the Kennedy era had passed by: "We're going to show these young people how to do things."

Eisenhower advised Johnson to speak for no more than ten minutes before a joint session of Congress. Johnson should note that he had "come to this office unexpectedly" and accepted "the decision of the Almighty." He should promise "no revolution in purpose or policy" —except to pursue a balanced budget. He should accept no resignations until after the "present period of emotional shock" was over. Eisenhower took the opportunity to complain of Kennedy's use of the Internal Revenue Service and Justice Department against his political enemies. After the Kennedy funeral, the General enjoyed a modest reconciliation over cocktails at the presidential guest quarters, Blair House, with Harry Truman, who told him, "I certainly don't go in for these Hollywood theatrics." Eisenhower agreed: "When I die, I want the cheapest casket there is—a sixty-dollar GI job and no medals on my chest."

As 1964 approached, Eisenhower realized that Senator Barry Goldwater of Arizona, who had once called his administration "a dime-store New Deal," might win the Republican nomination. This would be an ostentatious symbol of his failure to keep his party in moderate hands. He encouraged centrist Republicans like Governor William Scranton of Pennsylvania and Henry Cabot Lodge, now Ambassador to Saigon, to enter the Republican race. His unabated coolness toward Nelson Rockefeller kept him from aiding Goldwater's most powerful rival. Disarmed by friends who supported Goldwater, unwilling to openly take sides, Eisenhower refused to join what he called a "cabal" against the Arizonan. Those delegates who chose him would probably have denied it, but Goldwater's nomination was almost as great a repudiation of Eisenhower as Kennedy's victory in 1960. Like Kennedy's election and Nixon's renomination in 1956, had Eisenhower acted more decisively, he could have stopped it.

When he spoke to the 1964 convention, he electrifed the Goldwaterites with an aside against "sensation-seeking" journalists "who couldn't care less about the good of our party." (Someone cried, "Down with Walter Lippmann!") But the General's friend Ellis Slater found it "plain to see" that the delegates were "looking to new leaders. It's so often the case that a man who is a leader fades into dimness soon after he leaves the public scene."

197

June 1964: Eisenhower and Goldwater at a conference of American governors in Cleveland. The General did not block the nomination or influence the program of the Arizona senator who had called his administration a "dime-store New Deal."

In August, Goldwater went for a closed-door audience at Gettysburg, where Nixon heard the General "lay it on the line" in a way he had "seldom, if ever, heard." Eisenhower told Goldwater to "stop shooting from the hip"; he should publicly explain the alarming line in his acceptance speech that "extremism in the defense of liberty is no vice." The senator replied that his nature was not to be cautious: He could understand Eisenhower's sensitivity about any comments that might seem critical of his administration, but he meant "nothing personal." Then, at a press conference scheduled to allow Goldwater to blunt charges of extremism, Eisenhower winced as he heard the Senator make such statements as "I think Germany originated the modern concept of peace through strength." Afterwards he told friends, "I thought that Goldwater was just stubborn. Now I am convinced that he is just plain dumb."

Eisenhower was not altogether unhappy with the Johnson landslide. He was irritated by the President's commitment to expensive Great Society legislation and remained wary of his mercurial nature: "Johnson is unreliable and has no moral courage whatsoever." Warned by a friend that a Johnson landslide would reduce the President's backbone to stand up to organized labor, Eisenhower said, "He's never had any." But from his first day in office, Johnson had slathered the General with the ingratiating syrup that was one of his political specialties. From the White House to Gettysburg came dozens of the famous Johnson birthday, anniversary, and Christmas presents, including a tie clasp and wristwatch with an alarm device, both with the presidential seal. After years of presidential neglect, Eisenhower was not immune.

Johnson told the General after the 1964 election that he did not want to make a nuisance of himself, but if he got his "tail in a crack," he would "come running" to Eisenhower on foreign affairs. A birthday greeting: "Each passing day, we are stronger in purpose and firmer of faith for the unity we continue to find in your example and voice. You offer us the courage of the soldier and the counsel of the statesman. . . . But what we treasure most is your wise advice. . . . Your friendship will always be cherished." This was not the kind of letter Eisenhower had received from Kennedy.

As he prosecuted the war in Vietnam, Johnson needed the General's public support and wanted his private advice, sending General Goodpaster to brief him twice a month. Eisenhower told Johnson that, as with Korea in 1953, if the Chinese should threaten to intervene in the war, the United States should quietly "pass the word back to them to take care, lest dire results occur to them." He warned against gradual escalation of the fighting and excessive military decision making in Washington. The President should "untie" General William Westmoreland's hands: "When you once appeal to force in an international situation involving military help for a nation, you have to go all out! This is war, and . . . my advice is do what you have to do! . . . We are not going to be run out of a free country that we helped to establish."

In the air and in the family quarters and formal chambers of the White House *(this page and overleaf)*, President Johnson exerts himself in 1965 to keep the second most admired man in the country friendly—especially on Vietnam.

While advising Johnson, Eisenhower keeps his Republican fences mended, here at a Republican House of Representatives breakfast with Congressmen Gerald Ford of Michigan and Melvin Laird of Wisconsin.

The General lies in bed at Walter Reed Army Hospital, Washington, D.C., after his second heart attack, November 1965. He emerges a wizened version of the Eisenhower of old *(opposite)*.

Eisenhower complained to Robert Anderson in October 1966 of "the selfish and cowardly whimperings of some of these 'students' who —uninformed and brash though they are—arrogate to themselves the right to criticize, irresponsibly, our highest officials, and to condemn America's deepest commitments to her international friends." On television in November 1967, he argued that victory in Vietnam was still possible if there were changes in tactics and strategy. He recommended "hot pursuit" of enemy troops into Cambodia or Laos and dismissed those who were "talking about surrendering." He said, "If any Republican or Democrat suggests that we pull out of Vietnam and turn our backs on the more than thirteen thousand Americans who died in the cause of freedom there, they will have me to contend with."

One evening in November 1965, vacationing at their cabin on the Augusta National Golf Course in Georgia, he reminded Mamie that doctors had told him after his heart attack that he could expect an active life for as much as ten years. Now, he said, the ten years were up. The next day, he suffered a second coronary. After a slow recovery, he was able to resume golf, but only if he used a cart and played on par-three holes.

Now he knew that he was living on borrowed time. He gave up his Angus herd and began organizing his personal affairs. He approved plans for his state funeral, on which John had been secretly working with the Military District of Washington since 1962.

During the White House years, Eisenhower had told Ann Whitman that he supposed he and Mamie would be buried either at West Point, in Denver along with Mamie's family, or in Washington: No President had ever been buried at Arlington. Were it not for Kennedy's burial at Arlington, Eisenhower might have consented to burial there. But in 1965, acceding to requests from Kansas friends, he quietly decided on the non-sectarian Place of Meditation built next to his Abilene library: "Mamie and I thought it would be nice to be buried under the chapel instead of just having our headstone stuck up over our graves. That way, anybody taking the trouble to stop by would have a place to sit down."

In late 1967, he flew secretly to Kansas in an Army plane to watch his beloved son Icky's remains reinterred under the chapel floor. Afterwards Mamie called John from California to say that his father was ill in bed, his spirits very low. When Eisenhower suffered another heart attack the following spring, Mamie blamed it on his pain at seeing the tiny plaque on the floor with Icky's name and dates.

Early in 1968, Johnson golfed with Eisenhower at Palm Desert and afterwards wrote him, "I could not resist dropping in to draw on the strength of your wisdom and friendship again. . . . I will persevere, sustained by your support." In Vietnam, the Tet Offensive against the South reminded Eisenhower of the Battle of the Bulge, when he had asked for and won the reinforcements necessary for victory in Europe.

March 1967: At the
Eisenhower Medical Center,
Rancho Mirage, California, he
meets the new Governor of
California, Ronald Reagan.

Instead Johnson placed a ceiling on manpower commitments to Vietnam and announced on March 31 that he would drop out of the presidential race and stop the bombing of North Vietnam. With unprintable
language, Eisenhower expressed his fury that the President should now
cut and run. His close relations with Johnson abruptly ended. A month
later came the General's next heart attack. In May, he was brought
from California to Walter Reed Army Hospital in Washington, never
to emerge.

From the hospital Eisenhower followed the presidential campaign
of Richard Nixon, whose daughter Julie was now engaged to be married to his cherished grandson David. To prod Eisenhower into breaking his old tradition of endorsing no candidate before the convention,
Nixon asked the General's old friends Bryce Harlow and Lewis
Strauss, both veterans of the administration, to make the case. They
failed. In June, Eisenhower suffered another heart attack. In mid-July,
Nixon asked him outright and he relented: "Dick, I don't want there
to be any more question about this. You're my choice, period." He
promised to make a statement on August 5, the day the Republican
Convention was to open in Miami Beach.

Nixon gently asked him by letter to move up the timing: By opening day, it might be obvious that he had the nomination in his pocket.
Voters in the fall would not be impressed if Eisenhower had simply
ratified a fait accompli. The tired General had the cameras rolled into
his room. He told reporters that his endorsement was based on Nixon's
"intellect, acuity, decisiveness, warmth and, above all, his integrity."
The early endorsement irritated Milton Eisenhower, who years later

February 1968: Concerned that
Eisenhower is about to break
with him on Vietnam,
Johnson flies to Palm Desert
for golf, a game he does not
enjoy.

206

Returned to Walter Reed by another heart attack, the frail General receives President Johnson, their relations strained by Vietnam and 1968 presidential politics.

October 14, 1968: On his seventy-eighth birthday, Eisenhower waves his General of the Army's flag in response to an Army band serenade like the one after his ileitis attack thirteen years earlier.

noted that he himself had "never liked Nixon" and attributed his brother's break with custom to Mamie's intervention on Nixon's behalf. The episode created an historical symmetry: In 1960, Mamie's intervention had kept her husband from making the vital last campaign tour that would probably have won Nixon the election. This time, it was her intercession that helped Nixon to clinch the nomination.

Nixon found that Eisenhower was more than ever "obsessed with bringing younger people into government. . . . His close friends were all his age, but his protégés were invariably young." On Nixon's list of potential vice presidential candidates was the forty-four-year-old first-term Congressman from Texas, George Bush. In 1967 Eisenhower had told him that the son of his Connecticut friend, former Senator Prescott Bush, was a "comer."

At the start of convention week, Eisenhower dressed and briefly spoke to the delegates in Miami by television from Walter Reed. The next day, he suffered his sixth heart attack. In his acceptance speech, Nixon evoked a vast roar by crying, "Let's win this one for Ike!" Depressed, Eisenhower told intimates that death would be better than facing a future as a bedridden cripple and a burden to his family. A week later came another attack that nearly killed him. But once more he rebounded. A visitor that fall found that he had stuck Nixon buttons onto the electrodes affixed to his bare chest. In a letter he wrote: "I am still hopeful that one of these bright days I will be able to get around and mingle with my old friends, even though I think the verdict will be that I will never again play golf."

Flying from New York to Florida after his hairbreadth November victory over Hubert Humphrey, Nixon stopped in Washington to see his old chieftain: "Few moments in my life have been more satisfying then entering his room as the President-elect. . . . He urged me to describe for him every detail of the long election night and morning, and he beamed with pleasure all the while." Later that month, Eisenhower scrawled a telegram to the Army football coach before the Navy game: "My heart, though somewhat damaged, will be riding with you and the team." In December, he and Mamie watched his grandson's wedding to Julie Nixon on closed-circuit television. When Reverend

February 1969: The thirty-fourth and thirty-seventh Presidents, Walter Reed Army Hospital. Of their last visit a month after this photograph was taken, Nixon wrote: "I was so shocked at the deterioration of his condition that later I made a note, 'Looked like a corpse—waxen face.' As soon as he saw me, however, he brightened, raised his hand, and called out, 'Hi!' Even though it was visibly painful for him to talk, he insisted on having a conversation. 'You know, the doctors say I'm getting better,' he said. Always the optimist, perhaps he believed it."

Billy Graham came to visit, the General asked him with tears in his eyes, "Can an old sinner like me ever go to heaven?"

With an instinct for the fitting gesture, Nixon sent each member of his Cabinet to Walter Reed. Eisenhower said he was "quite anxious to meet the ones I do not know." The President-elect's new national security adviser, Henry Kissinger, who had never met the General, was startled by his intelligence and his "cold, deep blue, extraordinarily penetrating eyes." In February 1969, the doctors operated to remove scar tissue wrapped around Eisenhower's intestine, a vestige of the ileitis operation of 1956. The General told his son, "It's an eerie feeling to have them hit you with one thing and then another." John left "with a deep feeling of depression": It was "the first time Dad had ever uttered anything bordering on despair."

On March 24, the old man suffered progressive heart failure. With oxygen tubes in his nose and a filling of the lungs, he knew that this was going to be the end. He told John, "Be good to Mamie." On Friday morning, March 28, his wife of nearly fifty-three years, John, and grandson David stood around his bed, along with doctors and a nurse. The General cried out, "Lower the shades!" This done, he told John and one of the doctors, "Pull me up." They complied, but it was not enough. He glared from side to side: "Two big men—*higher.*" He looked at his son and softly said, "I want to go. God take me."

Shortly after noon, with Mamie holding his large hand and John and David standing at the corners of the bed, the signal on the electrocardiogram machine flickered away. After a moment, everyone left the room, but for some reason John felt compelled to return. When he did, he saw the screen register one final heartbeat. Then, almost immediately, he heard church bells tolling all over Washington.

Following his own strict instructions, the hero was placed in an eighty-dollar GI coffin. He wore the Army uniform he had not worn for seventeen years and, as he had promised Harry Truman, no medals on his chest. Drawn by horses, the black Lincoln catafalque took him to lie in state in the Capitol Rotunda, where President Nixon gave the eulogy, then to a funeral at the Washington Cathedral, attended by de Gaulle, the Shah of Iran, and Lyndon Johnson, who murmured his wish to be "as unobtrusive as possible" and slipped in and out through a side door. During the services, a grieving Milton Eisenhower collapsed.

At Union Station, the General's coffin was carried onto a train pulling the same Sante Fe car that had taken him to Abilene for his first address as a presidential candidate in June 1952. Over two days, hundreds and thousands waited along the route as the train rolled toward the heart of America. When the funeral coach arrived in Abilene, a pink sun glowed through clouds and a warm wind blew. Someone said it was "ideal plowing weather."

A military honor guard took him past the creamery where he had labored as a boy. (His portrait was displayed: "From the Belle Springs Icehouse to the White House—Ice Puller and Engineer Here 1906–

March 1969: Led by Lincoln's catafalque, the cortège moves up Capitol Hill along the same route on which Eisenhower was cheered after VE-Day and during his two inaugurals. In the Capitol Rotunda, President Nixon lays a wreath.

W ith Mamie and John
Eisenhower behind him,
Nixon delivers a eulogy.
During the Washington
Cathedral services, a frieze of
leaders: Nixon with his wife,
Pat, and daughter, Tricia, the
Shah of Iran, King Baudouin
of Belgium, President Habib
Bourguiba of Tunisia,
President Charles de Gaulle of
France.

1910".) A minister read from the Second Epistle of St. Paul: "I have fought a good fight. I have finished my course. I have kept the faith." Then he was buried near his infant son under the travertine floor of the chapel, near the stone museum built after the war, the stone library built after his Presidency, and the white clapboard house, now a shrine, all surrounded by rolling plains and what Eisenhower always called "the most beautiful region under God's blue sky."

On the day after Eisenhower's death, an aerial view of the Abilene monuments. At left is the homestead. At right, the presidential library. At bottom is the chapel Eisenhower helped to design. Here the General and President is buried alongside his infant son and his wife, who outlived him by a decade.

# 7.
# FALL AND RISE

During the last eight years of Dwight Eisenhower's life, Americans no longer seemed to consider him the commanding leader they had elected by the landslides of 1952 and 1956. According to the Gallup Poll, people still admired him more than almost anyone else in the country (from 1946 to 1969, he was consistently first or second on this list, except for 1964, when he was third). But politically they no longer seemed to take him seriously. As David Eisenhower lamented in a 1968 letter to Richard Nixon, "My Grandad is now regarded as a simple country bumpkin and a sweet old General."

In March 1969, a *New York Times* reporter who went to Times Square to conduct street interviews after Eisenhower's death heard the same kind of thing: "He was a great soldier. . . . As a President, he did the best he knew how. . . . He wasn't the greatest American President but everywhere he went, he improved our image in the world. . . . He was too nice a person to be a politician." What had happened?

One reason for the sagging respect for Eisenhower's political leadership during the 1960s was the deliberate effort of his successor. John Kennedy was too shrewd to lambast the beloved old General by name, but his 1960 campaign was chiefly a critique of the Eisenhower leadership: The United States was flagging in science, space, defense, world prestige; civil rights, poverty, housing, and other domestic problems had gone unaddressed; the U.S. President must be "in the thick of the fight"; it was "time to get this country moving again."

Kennedy did not have to force these ideas on a disbelieving public. *Sputnik* and fears about a Missile Gap had pierced the armor protecting Eisenhower's political reputation (just as the Iran-Contra scandal did Ronald Reagan's in 1986). People continued to love Eisenhower as they always had, but after these shocks, they were no longer resistant to Democratic charges that he was lazy, uninformed, not on top of his job, content to let the country slip into second place behind the Russians and brush social problems under the rug, where they festered and grew. Even Nikita Khrushchev, when he broke with Eisenhower after the U-2 affair, gibed: "The Americans themselves say their President has two jobs—golfing and being President. Which is the main one? *Playing golf!"*

Almost every newly elected President tries to improve his reputation by subtly deprecating the President who preceded him. (In 1988, George Bush owed his election to his predecessor perhaps more than any President since Taft, but he inevitably called attention to Ronald Reagan's flaws when he and his handlers made it clear that his would be a "kinder, gentler" country, that he would be a full-time, unscripted President who saw reporters without rehearsal, whose wife did not care about clothes, jewelry, and film stars, whose family gladly joined him for holidays.) Kennedy had much to gain from cutting his predecessor down to size. As long as Eisenhower remained a live, dominant political figure, glaring at him from Gettysburg and rousing voters against the New Frontier with speeches and television interviews, the young Democrat elected by such a slender margin would have trouble taking hold.

Establishing a favorable contrast to Eisenhower was one reason why the Kennedy entourage so heralded their man's energy, impatience, and rapid-fire speech, his speed reading and photographic memory, his demolition of the "unwieldy" existing presidential staff system to allow "activist leadership," his readiness to tackle problems long postponed. A week before Kennedy's inauguration, Richard Nixon complained to Christian Herter that "virtually everything this Administration has done has been brought into question or downgraded." Before long Eisenhower complained in private that Kennedy had become "the darling of the population." (He said this no doubt with wistful memories of the fifteen years after VE-Day.)

The General had high hopes that the first volume of his presidential memoirs would begin the renewal of his political standing. Instead, it became a metaphor for his eclipse by Kennedy. Published on November 9, 1963, *Mandate for Change* shot to second place on the *New York Times* bestseller list. Thirteen days later, Kennedy was murdered. The public no longer seemed interested in the man who had been the late President's most prominent public critic. Displaced by books eulogizing Kennedy, *Mandate* dropped off the charts.

Genuine history of a President and his administration cannot be written for at least a decade after he leaves office. Private letters and memoranda of Oval Office conversations remain sealed. Former officials are inclined to be guarded during interviews, if available at all. (Eisenhower's closest aide on foreign affairs, General Goodpaster, refused to speak to historians until the 1970s.) Too little time has passed to permit scholars to write with perspective. What was written about Eisenhower during the 1960s therefore was memoir and journalism. Neither was in his favor. The two best-known volumes of reminiscence published by Eisenhower aides at the time were Sherman Adams's *Firsthand Report* (1961), which had the effect of reminding people of the scandal that drove Adams from office, and *The Ordeal of Power* (1963), by Emmet John Hughes, a onetime Eisenhower speechwriter who had fallen out with him and now scored his "political naivete" and his administration's "film of irresolution and vacillation."

Eisenhower lacked Kennedy's foresight in choosing aides who had the ability and motivation to write graceful, highly persuasive books extolling their boss. In Arthur Schlesinger, Jr.'s, *A Thousand Days* (1965) and Theodore Sorensen's *Kennedy* (1965), read in excerpt or book form by millions of Americans, Eisenhower was the doddering antihero. Writing about Kennedy's Secretary of the Treasury, Douglas Dillon, Schlesinger observed that "the anomaly seemed to be, not that he was willing to join the Kennedy administration, but that he ever could have endured the Eisenhower administration. He used to describe the cabinet meetings—the opening prayer, the visual aids, the rehearsed presentations. 'We sat around looking at the plans for Dulles Airport. . . . [W]e would say why don't you put a door there, and they would explain why they didn't. It was great fun if you didn't have anything to do.' "

Those who wrote of the previous decade had to rely for source material on *The White House Years,* other memoirs, and published records such as the President's often inarticulate and intentionally unilluminating utterances in speeches and press conferences. They were deprived of the letters and minutes of secret meetings that were actually the best window on Eisenhower's mind and methods. They could not fail to be affected by what Garry Wills called the "spiked ozone" of the sixties, the enchantment with progressive, activist Presidents. Like Schlesinger, they saw Eisenhower as the image of inaction and the status quo. In his 1968 letter to Nixon, David Eisenhower complained that "the liberal element, since it does control educational and journalistic media to a vast degree," had "distorted" his grandfather's "personal and public image possibly forever." During the 1960s, Eisenhower was treated largely in the spirit of the columnist Marquis Childs's *Eisenhower: Captive Hero* (1958). Childs had not waited for Eisenhower to leave Washington to conclude that his "lack of knowledge and experience" had made the two terms "a national tragedy."

Another reason for Eisenhower's eclipse was iconographical. The old General seemed as alien to the youth-oriented culture of the sixties as Woodrow Wilson was to the roaring twenties. Linked in the public mind with Lawrence Welk, Grandma Moses, golf, and Big Business, openly scornful of abstract art, rock music, the twist, "kooks and hippies," he impressed many young Americans as a figure from a far-off place and time. Newspapers reported his displeasure with the length of his grandson's hair, which was short by the standards of the period. He underscored his standing as one of the most prominent "squares" of the era with his outspoken support of the war in Vietnam. Bizarrely, the man who had kept the nation out of foreign conflicts during the 1950s and fought the military-industrial establishment won a reputation for militarism. His granddaughter Susan was startled to be told by a classmate that her grandfather was a "warmonger."

Although Eisenhower was not a commanding figure in history during the 1960s, he might have been one in American politics. He was not. Republican leaders still loved the old General and were still eager to draw on his popularity, but many now took what political advice he gave them with a grain of salt, privately accepting the prevailing notion that he was a weak President or at best a blessed amateur. For them, Eisenhower had served his purpose: He had reclaimed the White House after twenty years of Democratic rule so that a more "genuine" Republican President could be elected in the future.

In 1964, the party drafted a platform that largely renounced the Eisenhower administration and chose the candidate who had uttered the words "dime-store New Deal." In 1968, when Richard Nixon asked Republicans to "win this one for Ike," he made no commitment to restore Eisenhower's approach to government. (Had Eisenhower known that as President, Nixon would authorize unbalanced budgets, wage and price controls, gradualism in Vietnam, and the acts that led to the Watergate scandals, he might never have endorsed him over other Republican possibilities.)

Eisenhower's meager political influence during the 1960s was largely his own doing. A final test of a President is what he does to ensure that his ideas and programs will live after he departs from active politics. No one did this better than Franklin Roosevelt. Through such efforts as his 1938 "purge" attempt against conservatives, FDR tried to make the Democrats a "really liberal party" that would carry on his agenda. He rarely left a thought unexpressed, and thus gave the nation a legacy of ideas, sometimes contradictory, usually stated in stirring rhetoric, which were cited and used by leaders and citizens of later generations. As the historian William Leuchtenburg has shown, the shadow of FDR fell across American politics for forty years and more after his death. Every Democratic nominee from Truman on explicitly tied himself to the Roosevelt tradition.

Eisenhower lacked Roosevelt's advantage of having been a heroic President in a heroic time, but why did his influence on American politics fade so quickly? One reason was the same distaste for political maneuvering that sometimes kept him from achieving important purposes while President. In the same way Eisenhower allowed Nixon to outfox him and stay on the 1956 ticket, he hamstrung his own efforts to work his will on the politics of the 1960s. In 1961 and 1962, he never gave the Republican Citizens the open, wholehearted support that might have made it a powerful engine for moderate Republicanism. In 1964, he cited his self-imposed rule against involvement in Republican presidential primaries, changed his mind, encouraging William Scranton to run, and then changed his mind again, pulling the rug out from under the moderate Governor of Pennsylvania.

The main reason for Eisenhower's flagging influence was more profound. Unlike Roosevelt and Democratic liberalism, he never made a thoroughgoing effort while President to turn the Republican Party into a permanent force for moderation in his own image. He always overestimated the capacity and willingness of the right wing to hurt him and thus never enlisted his vast popularity to take on the Old Guard once and for all. He never made a massive effort to reward and promote future leaders who were likely to act in his own tradition. One sign of the unreality with which Eisenhower thought about political heirs were his dreams about Milton Eisenhower and Robert Anderson ("Boy, I'd like to fight for him in 1960") as future Presidents. Whatever their virtues, these two men had virtually no chance of nomination or election, even in the event of his strong public endorsement.

Unlike Washington, Lincoln, Jefferson, and the two Roosevelts, Eisenhower resisted the idea that a President must be a teacher. He said privately in 1956 that what he meant to Americans was "sense and honesty and fairness and a decent amount of progress. I don't think the people *want* to be listening to a Roosevelt, sounding as if he were one of the Apostles." With few exceptions, such as his 1953 Chance for Peace speech and the Farewell Address, Eisenhower's presidential rhetoric was almost deliberately unmemorable. One result was that Americans in the 1960s who wished to emulate Eisenhower's example almost had to perform textual analysis upon his record of presidential decision making for the implicit values and attitudes that lay beneath it. His presidential memoir might have helped to correct the problem by setting out his credo, but *The White House Years* did not.

During his final years, Eisenhower was more philosophical about his reputation than Kennedy, who quizzed historians on what made a great President, or Johnson, who anticipated abuse by the "Harvards." Just before he left the White House, asked if over the years reporters had been fair to him, the General replied, "Well, when you come down to it, I don't see that a reporter could do much to a President, do you?"

His son John thought his father was far more concerned about his military reputation than what people said about his Presidency. Even in 1952, when he was about to become President, Eisenhower said, "I think I pretty well hit my peak in history when I accepted the German surrender." He was so stung by Viscount Montgomery's claim in his 1958 memoirs that the war could have been won in 1944 had Monty been in charge that he seriously considered suspending most of his presidential duties for two weeks to convene wartime aides "without wives" at Camp David, to "develop an agreed document" refuting Montgomery. For Eisenhower, the Supreme Command had been the peak of aspiration; the Presidency, so he always told himself, was "sheer duty."

In retirement, he was not above trying to fight defectors from his White House circle who wrote critical books, like Emmet John Hughes and E. Frederic Morrow, the first black White House staff member. When he learned about Hughes's contract with his own publisher, the General lambasted "you Doubleday people" for their alliance with someone "who writes books against me." (For whatever reason, the volume was removed to Atheneum.) Morrow was later convinced that Eisenhower's intervention kept his *Black Man in the White House* from being issued by a major publisher. Nevertheless, within the limits of his time and physical energy, Eisenhower was willing to be interviewed by anyone writing "honest history" about him, including high school students. Honoring the General's wishes, no presidential library has been more committed than the one at Abilene to opening its full archives to scholars as quickly as possible.

One reason why Eisenhower was relatively relaxed about his presidential reputation was his confidence that the more his record was studied, the better he would look to history. He was also shrewd enough to know that what historians said of his Presidency would be influenced more than a little by future currents of history and politics.

Among a series of "Afterthoughts" scrawled in the mid-1960s while completing *The White House Years,* Eisenhower wrote that if future Presidents followed "sound" fiscal policies and reduced government "intrusion" into private business, there would be "encomiums for my Administration as the first great break with the paternalistic philosophy of the two decades beginning in 1933." With foresight, he added that "if miraculously the Communists should one day renounce and abandon their objectives of world revolution and world domination," then "competent historians" would write that his "firm" policies "helped to bring about the Communist transformation."

Every generation uses history for its own purposes. Woodrow Wilson's priggishness, his belligerence toward business and toward foes of the League of Nations caused writers in the Dollar Decade of the twenties to write him off as hopelessly stubborn and dogmatic. World War II brought him back to life as a heroic man of principle celebrated in a Hollywood film. Historians of the 1950s once again found him a figure too rigid for his own good. By the 1960s, for some historians of the New Left, he had become an agent of corporate capitalism.

Having suffered its fall in the game of presidential chutes and ladders, Eisenhower's historical reputation began its rise around the time of his death. In a famous 1967 *Esquire* piece, the columnist Murray Kempton praised him as the "great tortoise on whose back the world sat for eight years," never appreciating the "cunning beneath the shell." At a time when Lyndon Johnson was mired in Vietnam and resolved not to be the "first American President to lose a war," Kempton found Eisenhower in retrospect to be "neither rash nor hesitant, free of the slightest concern for how things might look . . . as calm when he was demanding the wisdom of leaving a bad situation alone as when he was moving to meet it on those occasions when he absolutely had to."

The tragedies of Kennedy-Johnson activism in Indochina induced new esteem for a President who had been bold enough to resist demands for the overcommitment of American power in the world and to warn against the military-industrial complex. Inflation and the failures of Democratic social programs caused historians to show more respect than in the 1960s for a President who strove to balance his budgets and who was skeptical of government's ability to remake society. The deceptiveness and cynicism of Johnson and Nixon and their political self-destruction caused scholars to honor a kindly man of sound public ethics who managed to complete two terms and remain as popular as the day he began.

During the 1970s, the library in Abilene opened large portions of Eisenhower's letters, diaries, and other White House records. What these papers revealed most were Eisenhower's skills and methods. Memoranda of private Oval Office conversations showed that when behind closed doors, the Olympian, semiarticulate President of the press conferences was quick, deft, subtle, forceful, and manipulative—the product of wending his way up an Army hierarchy in which declarations of ideology and open personal conflict were penalized. Historians who had presumed that Eisenhower's foreign policy had been formed by John Foster Dulles and an elaborate West Wing "debating society" discovered that the President had made the main decisions and was only too happy to use Dulles or someone else as "prat boy" to take the blame for unpopular policies.

His speeches and public statements had led many scholars to believe that in making policy, his mind functioned on the level of platitude. His private letters showed that he brought to office a highly developed, coherent vision of American society and its role in the world. Domestically, this vision focused on a "corporate commonwealth," as the historian Robert Griffith called it, in which the President was driven to maintain the delicate balance among competing private interests. In the world, it was informed by the need to defend the West without spending the United States into bankruptcy, to prosecute the Cold War, and always to search for ways to relieve the dangers of confrontation and the arms race until the Soviets relaxed their ambitions.

The stage was set for a revisionist manifesto on Eisenhower, and in 1982 it came. In his book-length essay *The Hidden-Hand Presidency*, the Princeton political scientist Fred Greenstein (who had twice voted for Stevenson) made the most strenuous argument yet that Eisenhower was in fact a strong President. Greenstein used the newly opened material to show that "behind Eisenhower's seeming transcendence of politics was a vast amount of indirect, carefully concealed effort to exercise influence," employed to overcome the constitutional paradox by which a President is required to be both unifying chief of state and divisive political leader.

Greenstein's book implicitly nominated Eisenhower as Example A of a new model of strong presidential leadership, in counterpoint to that of the two Roosevelts, Truman, and other crusading Presidents celebrated by Richard Neustadt in his 1961 primer *Presidential Power*. Comparing Eisenhower to the Roosevelt model, other scholars had admonished him for failing to spend the political coin that his vast popularity gave him to enact a political program. Greenstein's book suggested that instead, Eisenhower had been an exemplary President for a time in which it is more important for a leader to unify and consolidate the American people than mobilize them for change.

As a political scientist mainly interested in Eisenhower's methods, Greenstein circumnavigated the problem of assessing his presidential policies and goals. This was done by the political and military historian Stephen Ambrose, also a Stevenson voter, whose two-volume biography *Eisenhower* appeared in 1983 and 1984. After reading Ambrose's life of General Henry Halleck in 1963, Eisenhower had invited him to be an editor of the Eisenhower papers being published by the Johns Hopkins University Press. In 1967, Ambrose published *Eisenhower and Berlin,* which was followed by *The Supreme Commander* (1970), and a history of Eisenhower's use of intelligence in war and peace, *Ike's Spies* (1981). Ambrose's biography became the central reference for scholars on Eisenhower. It concluded that, though hardly without flaws, this was a "great and good man," who had kept the peace, balanced the budget, stopped inflation, and maintained his popularity for eight years: "No wonder that millions of Americans felt that the country was damned lucky to have him."

Many historians of the time agreed. A poll of scholars in the 1980s found that Eisenhower's ranking among Presidents had ascended to ninth place. Still in 1986, Piers Brendon, a British historian and anti-monarchist (not inappropriate for an Eisenhower critic), weighed in with a skeptical volume stressing Eisenhower's "evasive straddling of the issues." Arthur Schlesinger, Jr., was willing to concede on the basis of the new scholarship "that behind the scene Eisenhower showed more energy, interest, purpose, cunning and command than many of us understood in the 1950s . . . and that the very talent for self-protection that led him to hide behind his reputation for muddle and to shove associates into the line of fire obscured his considerable capacity for decision and control." But he made it clear that he had not been seduced: "We were wrong to have underestimated Eisenhower's genius for self-presentation and self-preservation—the best evidence of which lies in his capacity to take in a generation of scholars."

Every careful student of history knows that no verdict is ever final. As scholars continue to scrutinize various facets of Eisenhower's career, his reputation as strategist, war leader, politician, overseer of the domestic economy, geopolitician, world crisis manager, and in other roles, his stock will move up and down on the historical exchange. The swings will probably be smaller and smaller as consensus forms. Judgments will be subject to new information, hindsight, fashion and, as Eisenhower himself was so aware, ideology.

Whatever the historical trends, it will be impossible to deny him much of the credit for the prosperity and near-peace that the United States enjoyed in the 1950s. His demands for balanced budgets saved the nation from the dangers of high inflation. His skill in defusing crises kept Vietnam, the Chinese offshore islands, Berlin, and other episodes from exploding into war. His scrutiny of military spending and his efforts to fan the embers of disarmament held the American-Soviet arms race to a lower level than might have been the case had he bent to partisan politics. Had it not been for the U-2 affair and the collapse of the Paris summit, he might have achieved a détente that could have helped to forestall the dangerous Cold War events of the early 1960s.

It is more difficult to argue on behalf of Eisenhower's approach to civil liberties. Many at the time not irrationally took his public silence on McCarthy to be acquiescence or even approval; had he spoken and acted more openly, he could have reduced the brutality of an ugly time. So too with civil rights: His nonchalance about the issue kept out of the debate what could have been a powerful voice in defense of principles of human equality for which World War II had been fought. Eisenhower himself might have argued in reply that, whatever his private views on these issues (and they were hardly passionate), it was more important for him not to jeopardize the national stature that endowed him with the political strength to make unpopular decisions on war and peace, standing up, as no other leader of the time could probably have done, to the demands for confrontation with the Russians and escalation of the arms race.

Harry Truman reputedly once recalled that after his nomination for Vice President in 1944, Franklin Roosevelt told him that it was not by accident that he had chosen him as a putative successor: After the exertions of the New Deal and world war, the nation would require more moderate and uneventful leadership. (The Truman years proved to be more momentous than Roosevelt might have imagined.)

During a period like the 1930s, requiring a President with an aggressive vision of government action and formidable skills for mobilizing the Congress and public behind it, Eisenhower would have been out of his element in the White House. But presuming that, as Roosevelt evidently believed, a period of turbulence and division must be followed by one of unity and rest, few could have been more fitted for that task in the 1950s than the World War II hero whose vast popularity muted political differences, and who restored the nation's morale and economy—an effort that ironically made Americans more receptive to the appeals for social reform that reached their crescendo after his Presidency.

Just as members of the Supreme Court are said to read the election returns, presidential candidates are not unaware of changing public tastes in their efforts to link themselves to great men of the past. In his uphill 1976 campaign, Gerald Ford compared himself to the surprise victor of 1948, the fighting Harry Truman, whose remembered honesty and "plain speaking" had brought him into vogue after Watergate. In 1980, seeking votes of independents and labor Democrats, Ronald

Reagan cast himself as the new Franklin Roosevelt. When Senator Gary Hart of Colorado ran in the Democratic primaries of 1984, political reporters lampooned his efforts to style his looks and rhetoric (and some said, his private life) after Kennedy's.

As candidate and as President, Ronald Reagan did little to compare himself to the last Republican to serve two terms in the White House, but he benefited from the new historical esteem for Eisenhower. In 1980, Lance Morrow wrote in *Time* that Americans trying to picture a Reagan administration "sometimes find their minds drifting back to the 1950s. Ike, they tell themselves. Maybe if he won, Ronald Reagan would turn into a kind of Eisenhower. Or at any rate, maybe the effect would be the same: a long quiescence, an essentially sane and minimalist White House presiding over a 'normality' that the nation has not experienced for a generation. Even some voters who are chilled by Reagan's politics and his followers have begun to take wistful consolation in the thought that the future under Reagan might be a kind of doubling back to the simpler past of the '50s: not the most ennobling American era, they admit, but not such a bad one either. Worse things have happened, such as twenty years of assassinations, riots, Vietnam and Watergate, OPEC's extortions and the dollar's humiliation. *Après Ike, le deluge.* Eisenhower's '50s begin to seem an almost golden time."

That subliminal longing for Eisenhower and the tranquility and national consensus of the 1950s was an important reservoir of goodwill toward Reagan throughout his eight years. Popular culture holds a mirror to the national psyche: It was not by coincidence that the fashions of the eighties in clothing, food, music, art, architecture, and design were largely the fashions of the fifties. After the thwarted tenures of every President since Eisenhower, there was a profound, almost patriotic conviction that the nation should allow one of its Presidents to complete two terms and leave office in the kind of popular glow Eisenhower had enjoyed in 1961. One reason Reagan ran for reelection in 1984 was his feeling that the nation needed to have a two-term Presidency. He found this reservoir of goodwill especially helpful during the Iran-Contra scandal: Congressional leaders did not seem to have the stomach to consider throwing another President out of office.

Reagan benefited from Eisenhower's historical resurgence in another way. If scholars now revered a President who relied heavily on his staff and did not try to "micromanage," whose impromptu public utterances were often indistinct, who took much time off for relaxation, why should they not admire Reagan? Perhaps in twenty years, they would find that Reagan too was a "hidden-hand" President whose vague public manner concealed private skills of quickness and command. At the very least, historians and journalists who believed Eisenhower had been misunderstood during his Presidency now thought twice before saying that Reagan was merely the actor-front man for a hyperactive staff that ran the country.

In 1980, when Jimmy Carter intoned that being President was a "full-time job" and his handlers ran commercials of him working late at night in the Oval Office, Reagan successfully retorted that any President who worried about who was "playing on the White House tennis court" was not a good manager. In 1984, Walter Mondale's complaints that Reagan "does not know those things that a President must know" fell on deaf ears. The Iran-Contra affair should have demonstrated the dangers of a President who seems not to know what is being done in his name. Eisenhower's recognition of this danger was one reason why he took the blame for sending the U-2 over Russia on May Day, 1960. But it was Reagan's claim that he did not know about the arms-for-hostages trade that kept him from being immolated by the scandal.

On the rare occasions when he mentioned Eisenhower's name in public, Reagan used the General mainly for rhetorical flourishes. He noted Eisenhower's observations that freedom "must be daily earned and refreshed"; that the start of human cooperation was "genuine, human understanding"; that American foreign policy could be summarized as "we are for peace first, last and always"; that farming looked easy when you were a thousand miles from a cornfield and your plow was a pencil. Indeed, Eisenhower had said all of these things, but they had little to do with his most deeply felt beliefs and could have been said by almost any President.

On the occasion Reagan came closest to citing Eisenhower on substance, he used him, of all things, to defend his massive defense buildup and budget deficits. During a January 1983 press conference, asked if he might possibly "stretch out" his defense buildup to reduce the huge deficits, Reagan replied: "A stretch-out sounds as if it might not be too serious, but you have to remember we don't have the military-industrial complex that we once had when President Eisenhower spoke about it. Assembly lines had to be put together and started up again [in 1980 and 1981] to meet the demand for the weapons system. Now you can't say to someone who has gone into business purely to provide us with what we've produced—you can't suddenly say to him, 'Well, now, everybody go home and wait awhile. We're not going to take these things.'"

Reagan's foes borrowed from Eisenhower with finer historical accuracy, citing his Chance for Peace speech and his lament about national bankruptcy induced by indiscriminate Pentagon spending: "God help the nation when it has a President who doesn't know as much about the military as I do." It took no Einstein to figure out which President they had in mind. In a Capitol Hill ballroom in January 1986, a group of businessmen concerned about excessive military spending convened a glittering array of dinner guests from the Eisenhower administration and family to celebrate the twenty-fifth anniversary of the General's warning against the military-industrial complex.

In 1988, as more than one journalist noted, Reagan's situation was strangely reminiscent of Eisenhower's in 1960. Hoping to begin winding down the Cold War, a weary President was going to Moscow for talks with the Soviet leader. Then his Vice President would campaign to succeed him, against a Massachusetts Democrat and his older Texas running mate. George Bush may have been more reminded of 1960 than he wished to be. Like Eisenhower, Reagan refused to get involved in Republican primaries and, once his Vice President had won the nomination, delivered no more than a perfunctory public endorsement. That fall, Bush's managers reminded Reagan that Eisenhower's seemingly halfhearted support may have cost Nixon the 1960 election. This moved the President to be more involved in the fall campaign than Eisenhower had ever been, even to the point of inviting Bush to suggest end-of-term appointments to the Reagan Cabinet.

The result was that as 1990 and the centennial year of Eisenhower's birth began, the sitting President of the United States was a man with strong political roots in the Eisenhower era. George Bush's father was one of the northeastern Republicans who had gone to Paris to ask the General to run for President: Prescott Bush was elected Senator from Connecticut in the first Eisenhower landslide. The senior Bush was a favorite presidential golfing partner and ranked high when Eisenhower once scrawled a list of fourteen possible candidates to succeed him.

Those years doubtless left a strong impression on the son. Eisenhower was the first President for whom George Bush voted. Announcing his first national candidacy in May 1979, he twice quoted his father's hero (calling for "a middle way between the untrammeled freedom of the individual and the demands for welfare of the whole nation" and "a leadership confident of its strength, compassionate of heart and clear of mind"). During the 1980s, as he wooed the conservatives who dominated his party, it was scarcely in his interest to emphasize his ties to the symbol of more moderate Republicanism. But in the White House, Bush resembled no President more than Eisenhower in his muted rhetoric, his reliance on staff, his emphasis on teamwork within the Executive Branch and with Congress, his temperamental resistance to the ideology of right or left. In September 1989, the *Washington Post* political writer David Broder noted the parallel in a column entitled "Eisenhower Lives."

Part of Eisenhower's continuing political life are those elements of his political leadership that are particularly useful to remember in the 1990s. As the Cold War falls away, Eisenhower deserves the same credit as every President since 1945 for mobilizing a traditionally isolationist people to make painful sacrifices for defense at the same time as he kept alive the hope for an American-Soviet accommodation and averted nuclear war. But of the Cold War Presidents, Eisenhower was the one who worried most that the "military-industrial-Congressional complex" would generate its own Cold War momentum, and that endless spending for a national security state would bankrupt the nation and deplete its ability to exercise positive influence in the world. Americans would do well to recall the political bravery of his second term, when he resisted pressures to spend more than he deemed necessary on the Pentagon and thus deplete the nation's economic strength.

They should also remember Eisenhower's restraint and gift for taking the fever out of crisis. He would have recoiled from the notion of exploiting foreign challenges like Quemoy-Matsu, Lebanon, or Berlin to rally support for himself among the voters or in Congress. It was not coincidental that during Eisenhower's eight years, many troubled places that could have erupted in crisis did not. This was in sharp contrast to the later practice of viewing episodes like the Iran hostage crisis and Grenada almost as much in terms of driving up the President's domestic popularity as in terms of the actual danger to the nation's security.

Americans would also benefit from recalling Eisenhower's political persona in this age of political "programming" by consultants and pollsters. This is not to say that he disdained modern techniques: He was the first presidential candidate to hire a full-time Madison Avenue firm and the first President to hire a television adviser to oversee makeup and lighting. But Eisenhower would never have dreamed of consulting political advisers before making a speech on foreign policy or checking overnight poll results, in the manner of some of his successors. More than once he expelled an aide from the Oval Office for presuming to advise him about an issue's ramifications on a forthcoming election. Milton Eisenhower recalled his brother's general view: "If an essential policy or decision happened to have a bad political effect, too damn bad. . . . He really had enough confidence in the American people that he believed that they would accept the truth and then act wisely."

This was part of a political self-confidence that is often absent from the leaders of our own time. It was intertwined with those other qualities that were the best of Eisenhower's political personality—his optimism, civility, honesty, goodwill, and genuine sense of duty. Although capable of private animosity and sometimes pettiness (against Truman, Stevenson, and Kennedy, for instance), he obeyed his own rule against public attacks on personalities. Unlike later Presidents who set members of their staffs against one another, Eisenhower's approach in the West Wing was what it had been during the war: "I want to see a big crowd of friends around here." One reason for this manner of politics was his essential kindliness, another his belief that collaboration achieved more than competition. Most important of all was the fact that he had a life and a history that lay beyond the realm of politics: More than most national leaders of our own day, Eisenhower in political defeat would have been relatively serene in returning to private life.

H is nonchalance about how historians would remember his White House years was in the main authentic. But just as while President he pulled more of the strings than almost anyone knew, he was not willing to leave his historical reputation entirely to fate. Buried inside one of the brick chimneys of the farmhouse at Gettysburg, now a National Historic Site, is a copper box Eisenhower quietly installed while President, telling almost no one. Sealed inside the copper box, alongside artifacts of his life and work, are two documents. The few who know about them at first hand believe the first to be his no-holds-barred assessment of the Allied officers who served under him in World War II. The second is evidently a message to Americans of the future on the politics of the United States and the world.

Under Eisenhower's precise stipulation, his private time capsule will not be opened until well into the twenty-first century. Whatever future historians write of his career, the Supreme Allied Commander and thirty-fourth President of the United States has ensured that he will have at least the near-to-last word.

# ACKNOWLEDGMENTS

When I set out to write the text and captions and to oversee the selection of photographs for this volume, my esteemed publisher, Edward Burlingame, promised expert assistance to an historian normally accustomed to writing much longer works of prose. Thus the book has gained from Vincent Virga's mastery of photographic archives and from Joel Avirom's expertise in book design. Thanks are also due to Joseph Montebello, who governed the synthesis of word and picture, and Christa Weil, who ensured that the entire process moved smoothly. Maryam Mashayekhi helped to assemble research materials in Washington. John Wickman, Mack Teasley, David Haight, Kathy Struss, Hazel Stroda and other members of the staff of the Eisenhower Library assisted all who worked on this book with their customary high professionalism. I am also grateful to two friends who scrutinized the manuscript—James MacGregor Burns, a member of the opposition during the Eisenhower years, and Stephen E. Ambrose, who gave the text the immense benefit of his three decades of Eisenhower scholarship.

—Michael R. Beschloss
Washington, D.C.

# SOURCE NOTES ON THE TEXT
BY PAGE

## 1. "CHANCE ARRANGEMENT OF FATE"

17 *Late nineteenth-century Abilene:* Peter Lyon, *Eisenhower* (Little, Brown, 1974), p. 37; Stephen E. Ambrose, *Eisenhower: Soldier, General of the Army, President-Elect* (Simon & Schuster, 1983), pp. 23–27.

*Grandparents' migration:* Kenneth S. Davis, *Soldier of Democracy* (Doubleday, 1945), pp. 18–19.

*David Eisenhower's bankruptcy:* Dwight D. Eisenhower, *At Ease* (Doubleday, 1967), pp. 32–33.

18 *Eisenhower on Pentagon office:* Eisenhower, *At Ease*, p. 73.

*"I got something"* and *"Dad cried":* Merle Miller, *Ike the Soldier* (Putnam, 1987), p. 69.

*"Thieves, embezzlers":* Eisenhower, *At Ease*, p. 32.

*"The most to learn":* Eisenhower, *At Ease*, p. 52.

*Friend on Eisenhower's "unloosened energy":* William Robinson, quoted in William B. Ewald, *Eisenhower the President* (Prentice-Hall, 1981), p. 42.

18–19 *Eisenhower on Halloween 1900:* Eisenhower, *At Ease*, pp. 51–52.

19 *Eisenhower on never knowing he was poor: New York Times*, 6/5/52.

*"They'd make us feel":* Lyon, p. 40.

*David on standing up for rights:* Eisenhower to Bela Kornitzer, notes from tape recording, 12/1/53, Dwight D. Eisenhower Library, hereafter DDEL.

*"I never heard a cross":* Eisenhower, *At Ease*, p. 37.

*"Opportunity is all around": New York Times*, 6/5/52.

*Eisenhower on father's ambition:* Eisenhower to Kornitzer, 12/1/53, DDEL.

19–20 *Eisenhower on George Washington:* Eisenhower, *At Ease*, pp. 40–41.

20 *"I could not imagine":* Eisenhower, *At Ease*, p. 96.

*Eisenhower on black football opponent:* Ambrose, *Eisenhower: Soldier*, pp. 34–35.

*Eisenhower's application and admission to West Point:* Eisenhower, *At Ease*, pp. 103–8.

*Milton on Ida's reaction to Dwight's departure:* Eisenhower, *At Ease*, p. 108.

*West Point creed and atmosphere:* Ambrose, *Eisenhower: Soldier*, pp. 44–48, 53; Ambrose, *Duty, Honor, Country* (Johns Hopkins, 1966); Lyon, pp. 43–48.

*"One of the most promising backs":* Robert F. Burk, *Dwight D. Eisenhower* (Twayne, 1986), p. 19.

*"I was almost despondent":* Eisenhower, *At Ease*, p. 16.

234

**20–21** *"Stupid and unforgivable"* and *"For the first time"*: Eisenhower, *At Ease*, p. 18.

**21** *Eisenhower to Ruby Norman on Christmas leave* and *"Seems like I'm never cheerful"*: Eisenhower to Ruby Norman, undated, DDEL.

**24** *"More than ever now I want"* and *"Your love is my whole world"*: Miller, pp. 126–28.

**24–25** *"Woman-hater"* and *"Saucy in the look"*: Eisenhower, *At Ease*, p. 113.

**25** *"The girl I run around"*: Miller, pp. 129–30.

*"At last I have"*: Ambrose, *Eisenhower: Soldier*, p. 59.

*Ruby Norman's daughter's comment*: Miller, pp. 130–31.

*Gladys's note on love letters*: Miller, p. 132.

*"All those lounge lizards"*: Julie Nixon Eisenhower, *Special People* (Simon & Schuster, 1977), p. 195.

*"Mamie could have done"*: Lester and Irene David, *Ike and Mamie* (Putnam, 1981), p. 59.

*"Ike never told me"*: Julie Eisenhower, p. 196.

**25–28** *"Mamie told me"* and *"Mamie and Ike sat around"*: Howard Snyder Diary, 1/18/60 and 5/8/60, DDEL.

**28** *"I never got used"*: Steve Neal, *The Eisenhowers* (Doubleday, 1978), p. 42.

*"Smoothing the edges"*: Neal, p. 38.

*"My country comes first"*: Julie Eisenhower, p. 197.

*"One of the greatest soldiers"*: Davids, p. 76.

*"The greatest disappointment"*: Eisenhower, *At Ease*, p. 181.

*Eisenhower on daffodils*: Robert J. Donovan, *Confidential Secretary* (Dutton, 1988), p. 45.

*"A tragedy from which we never"*: Eisenhower, *At Ease*, p. 181.

*"Makes one wonder whether"*: Dwight D. Eisenhower Diaries, hereafter DDED, 12/2/47, DDEL.

*"Two young people who were"*: Davids, p. 90.

*"Did much to fill the gap"*: Eisenhower, *At Ease*, p. 194.

**29** *Eisenhower on tutelage under Conner*: Eisenhower, *At Ease*, pp. 182–87.

*"One of the most profound"*: Eisenhower, *At Ease*, p. 195.

*"You are far better"*: Eisenhower, *At Ease*, p. 201.

*"Where I was supposed to command"*: Eisenhower to Andrew Goodpaster, 3/3/62, DDEL.

**30** *"Please don't go"*: Lyon, p. 64.

*"A hell of an intellect"* and *"With that dramatic"*: Lyon, p. 69.

*"Clean-cut line between the military"*: Eisenhower, *At Ease*, p. 213.

*"What the hell are you talking"*: Ambrose, *Eisenhower: Soldier*, p. 96.

**30–31** *"While I have no definite leanings"*: DDED, 2/28/33.

**31** *"It would have been a wonderful"*: Eisenhower to Andrew Goodpaster, 3/3/62, DDEL.

*Eisenhower to Quezon's main desire*: Lyon, p. 77.

*"Jim and I undertook"*: DDED, 5/29/36.

*"TJ and I came in"*: DDED, 9/26/36.

**33** *MacArthur-Eisenhower exchange on Manila parade*: Lyon, p. 79.

**33–34** *"During all those years"*: Eisenhower to Andrew Goodpaster, 3/3/62, DDEL.

**34** *"Happy in my work"*: Eisenhower, *At Ease*, p. 241.

*"The United States cannot remain"* and *MacArthur, Quezon requests to stay*: Eisenhower, *At Ease*, p. 231.

*"We're going to fight . . . Such great expenditures"*: Ambrose, *Eisenhower: Soldier*, p. 124.

*"A God-awful spot"*: Ambrose, *Eisenhower: Soldier*, p. 128.

*Eisenhower on December 7, 1941*: Eisenhower, *At Ease*, p. 245.

## 2. NEITHER NAPOLEON NOR CAESAR

37  *"It's hard as hell"*: Theodore H. White, ed., *The Stilwell Papers* (Sloane, 1948), p. 21.

*Eisenhower and Marshall on December 14*: Dwight D. Eisenhower, *Crusade in Europe* (Doubleday, 1948), pp. 16–22.

38  *"Looks like MacArthur"*: DDED, 2/3/42.

*"Bataan is made"*: DDED, 2/23/42.

*Eisenhower on father's death*: DDED, 3/10/42–3/12/42.

*Eisenhower on Marshall*: Ambrose, *Eisenhower: Soldier*, pp. 135–36.

*"I know that you were recommended"* and *"If that locks me . . . Anger cannot win"*: Ambrose, *Eisenhower: Soldier*, p. 143.

*Eisenhower's promotion to major general*: Ambrose, *Eisenhower: Soldier*, p. 144.

40  *"Slugging with air"*: Ambrose, *Eisenhower: Soldier*, p. 147.

*Roosevelt on Eisenhower's capacity*: William Manchester, *The Glory and the Dream* (Little, Brown, 1975), p. 276.

*Eisenhower's appointment to London*: DDED, 6/6/42, 6/11/42.

*"Happy family"* and *"I want to see"*: Stephen E. Ambrose, *The Supreme Commander* (Doubleday, 1970), pp. 55–56.

*"I love that man"*: Robert Cutler, *No Time for Rest* (Little, Brown, 1966), p. 264.

*"It was not long before one"*: Ambrose, *The Supreme Commander*, p. 97.

*"Quasi-members"*: Harry Butcher, *My Three Years with Eisenhower* (Simon & Schuster, 1946), p. 20.

41  *"Big Brass"* and *"When they called me Uncle"*: Lyon, p. 268.

*"I'll make the son of a bitch"*: Ambrose, *The Supreme Commander*, p. 88.

42  *"Something of a quite desperate nature"*: DDED, 9/2/42.

*"The symbol of the solidity"*: DDED, 11/9/42.

*"Unsure of himself"*: Ambrose, *The Supreme Commander*, p. 137.

*"In the long run, we could defeat"*: Eisenhower, *At Ease*, pp. 255–56.

45  *"I have been called a Fascist"*: Eisenhower to John Eisenhower, 12/20/42, DDEL.

*"I can't understand"*: Harold Macmillan, *Blast of War* (Macmillan, 1967), pp. 220–21.

*"Anything for the battle, but"*: Miller, p. 429.

*Marshall's Christmas 1942 order, rumors of Eisenhower losing job, and "Ike seems jittery"*: Ambrose, *Eisenhower: Soldier*, p. 215–28.

*"Whole attitude toward Ike"*: Butcher, p. 247.

46  *"Are now mad and ready"*: Ambrose, *Eisenhower: Soldier*, p. 231.

*"I only wish"*: John S. D. Eisenhower, ed., *Letters to Mamie* (Doubleday, 1978), p. 118.

*Macmillan on North African victory*: Macmillan, p. 325.

*Gladys Brooks to Eisenhower*: Miller, p. 502.

49  *"Our relationships seemed"*: Kay Summersby Morgan, *Past Forgetting* (Simon & Schuster, 1976), p. 172.

*"Stop worrying about me"*: Davids, p. 159.

49–55  *Eisenhower's hopes for Sicily*: Eisenhower, *Crusade*, pp. 159–62.

55  *Eisenhower and Italian surrender*: Ambrose, *Eisenhower: Soldier*, pp. 248–66.

60 *"I hate to think"*: Eisenhower, *Crusade,* p. 197.

*Command of Overlord established:* John S. D. Eisenhower, *Allies* (Doubleday, 1982), pp. 371–74, 386–401, 408–24.

61 *"A gigantic job"*: Miller, p. 560.

*"Don't come back until"*: Ambrose, *Eisenhower: Soldier,* p. 280.

63 *"Ike looks worn"*: Ambrose, *Eisenhower: Soldier,* p. 292.

*Stagg to Eisenhower on D-Day weather:* Eisenhower, *Crusade,* pp. 249–50.

*"The question is just"*: Ambrose, *The Supreme Commander,* p. 416.

*"Loneliness and isolation"*: Ambrose, *Eisenhower: Soldier,* p. 308.

*Eisenhower orders Overlord to begin:* John Eisenhower, *Allies,* pp. 468–69.

66 *"Thank the gods of war"*: Ambrose, *Eisenhower: Soldier,* p. 312.

*"My mind goes back"*: Miller, p. 618.

*"Unbalancing the enemy"* and *"Persuade Monty"*: Ambrose, *Eisenhower: Soldier,* pp. 315, 318.

*"The heaviest and most concentrated"*: Forrest C. Pogue, *The Supreme Command* (Department of the Army, 1954), p. 188.

*Eisenhower order to Patton's forces:* Ambrose, *Eisenhower: Soldier,* p. 325.

*"Fight to the bitter"*: Butcher, pp. 644–46.

69 *"People of the strength"*: Ambrose, *Eisenhower: Soldier,* p. 357.

*Eisenhower-Montgomery differences over Bulge:* Ambrose, *Eisenhower: Soldier,* pp. 368–80.

*Eisenhower's insistence on Transportation Plan:* Ambrose, *Eisenhower: Soldier,* pp. 286–90.

71 *"A pretty stiff price"*: Omar Bradley, *A Soldier's Story* (Holt, 1951), p. 535.

71–82 *Eisenhower and Berlin:* Ambrose, *Eisenhower: Soldier,* pp. 392–96, 403–4; David Eisenhower, *Eisenhower: At War* (Random House, 1986), pp. 712–13, 727–33, 742–43, 751–52, 768–69.

82 *"I never dreamed"* and *"The things I saw"*. Ambrose, *Eisenhower: Soldier,* p. 400.

*Eisenhower and German prisoners:* James Bacque, *Other Losses* (Stoddert, 1989); Stephen E. Ambrose, "Eisenhower and the 'Other Losses,' " unpublished article.

*German surrender:* Ambrose, *Eisenhower: Soldier,* pp. 405–8.

*"Greatest outburst of joy"*: Winston S. Churchill, *Triumph and Tragedy* (Houghton, 1953), p. 548.

## 3. "A KIND OF DREAM BOY"

85 *"The greatest strategist"*: Lyon, p. 7.

*Eisenhower to Truman on Bomb:* Dwight D. Eisenhower, *The White House Years: Mandate for Change* (Doubleday, 1963), pp. 312–13.

*"If we have to fight"*: Ambrose, *Eisenhower: Soldier,* p. 429.

*Eisenhower in Moscow after Bomb:* Lyon, p. 356.

85–87 *"When this hectic war"*: John Eisenhower, *Letters to Mamie,* p. 157.

87 *"He belonged to the world"*: Julie Eisenhower, p. 202.

*"The taste of it I had"*: Eisenhower, *At Ease,* p. 316.

*"This job (chief of staff)"*: DDED, 12/15/45.

*Eisenhower on Truman's 1945 offer:* Eisenhower, *Crusade,* p. 444.

87–91 *"A number of well-meaning"*: DDED, 11/12/46.

91–92 *"This will lead"* and *Eisenhower's reply:* Miller, p. 20.

**92** *"Justified on his human qualities":* Ronald Steel, *Walter Lippmann and the American Century* (Atlantic Little, Brown, 1980), p. 481.

*Eisenhower on Roosevelt:* Ewald, pp. 24–27.

*"A fine man who":* DDED, 11/6/50.

**93** *Eisenhower on patronage:* DDED, 1/5/53.

*"The voteseeker rarely hesitates":* Robert Griffith, "Dwight D. Eisenhower and the Corporate Commonwealth," *American Historial Review,* 2/82.

*"A combination of gossip":* Eisenhower to Edgar Eisenhower, 1/27/54, DDEL.

*"I won't drag this uniform":* Theodore H. White, *In Search of History* (Harper & Row, 1978), p. 350.

*"Extremes on the right":* Ewald, p. 44.

*"A terrific popular pressure":* Eisenhower to Milton Eisenhower, 10/16/47, DDEL.

**94** *"You don't suppose":* Steel, p. 481.

*Royall's offer:* Lyon, p. 377.

*Eisenhower's private views on 1948:* Ewald, p. 184.

*"Completely taken me":* DDED, 12/31/47.

*Fee for* Crusade: Lyon, p. 375.

*Eisenhower on Crusade sales:* Howard Snyder Diary, 3/29/60, DDEL.

**96** *"In a way it was a 'stampeding' ":* DDED, 7/24/47.

*"Columbia is the place":* DDED, 1/1/50.

**96–98** *"The governor says":* DDED, 7/7/49.

**98–100** *"I do not think it is particularly":* DDED, 10/28/50.

**100** *"I rather look upon this effort":* Eisenhower to Everett Hazlett, 11/1/50, DDEL.

*Eisenhower-Taft meeting before departure for Europe:* Eisenhower, *At Ease,* pp. 371–72.

**100–101** *McCall's offer.* Lyon, p. 430.

**101** *Lodge-Eisenhower September 1951 meeting:* Ambrose, *Eisenhower: Soldier,* p. 516.

**101–103** *"The temptation grows":* DDED, 10/4/51.

**103** *"Any personal sacrifice,"* Lodge *December warning,* and *"The seeker is never":* Ambrose, *Eisenhower: Soldier,* pp. 518–21.

*"Time and time again":* DDED, 1/10/52.

*"To place before me":* New York Times, 1/8/52.

**106** *Cochran on evening with Eisenhowers:* Jacqueline Cochran oral history, DDEL.

*"Brought home to me":* Eisenhower to Hazlett, 2/12/52, DDEL.

*Eisenhower's intention to return to campaign:* Jacqueline Cochran oral history, DDEL.

*"Ike Is Back":* New York Times, 6/5/52.

*"I hope I never get pontifical"* and *"We are, of course":* New York Times, 6/5/52.

**108** *Nixon in caucus:* Roger Morris, *Richard Milhous Nixon* (Holt, 1990), pp. 676–736.

**109** *Eisenhower acceptance speech:* New York Times, 7/12/52, and audiotape of speech in DDEL.

*Stevenson and Eisenhower preference for other opponents:* Lyon, p. 449fn; John Bartlow Martin, *Adlai Stevenson of Illinois* (Doubleday, 1977), p. 567.

*Eisenhower "liberation" demand:* Ambrose, *Eisenhower: Soldier,* pp. 546–48.

*Nixon on "College":* Morris, pp. 861–62.

**109–110** *Eisenhower-Taft breakfast and Stevenson quip:* Lyon, pp. 451–52; Martin, pp. 675–76.

**110** *Eisenhower appearances with Jenner and McCarthy:* Ambrose, *Eisenhower: Soldier,* pp. 552–53, 563–67.

**111** *"Checkers" episode:* Ambrose, *Eisenhower: Soldier,* pp. 553–61.

*Eisenhower's campaign method:* Fred Greenstein, *The Hidden-Hand Presidency* (Basic, 1982), p. 38.

**115** *Eisenhower's Korea pledge and its effect:* Ambrose, *Eisenhower: Soldier,* pp. 569–70.

## 4. MANDATE

**119** *"My first day":* DDED, 1/21/53.

*"Greater serenity and confidence":* Walter Cronkite interviews with Eisenhower, CBS Television, 1961 DDEL.

*"Russia has not":* Lyon, p. 395.

*"Feeling of depression":* Eisenhower, *Mandate for Change,* p. 312.

*"There is not one disputed":* Robert A. Divine, *Eisenhower and the Cold War* (Oxford, 1981), p. 107.

**121** *"Look, I am tired":* Emmet John Hughes, *The Ordeal of Power* (Atheneum, 1963), p. 103.

*"Every gun that is fired":* Dwight D. Eisenhower, *Public Papers of the Presidents,* hereafter DDEPP (U.S. Government Printing Office, 1954–1961), 4/16/53.

*"As of now, the world":* DDED, 10/10/53.

**122** *"Today, the United States stockpile":* DDEPP, 12/8/53.

*"Chip in the granite":* Dwight D. Eisenhower, *The White House Years: Waging Peace* (Doubleday, 1965), p. 432.

**123** *Nuclear threat on Korea:* McGeorge Bundy, *Danger and Survival* (Random House, 1988), pp. 238–245.

*Nuclear threat and Vietnam:* Bundy, pp. 260–270.

*"You boys":* Stephen E. Ambrose, *Eisenhower: The President* (Simon & Schuster, 1984), p. 184.

**124** *"I have come to the conclusion":* Eisenhower to Lewis Douglas, 3/29/55, DDEL.

**126** *"To induce people":* Griffith, *American Historical Review,* 2/82.

*"Should any political party":* Eisenhower to Edgar Eisenhower, 11/8/54, DDEL.

*"Whenever the President takes part":* Eisenhower to Hazlett, 7/21/53, DDEL.

*"I just won't get":* Piers Brendon, *Ike* (Harper & Row, 1986), p. 13.

**127** *"Senator McCarthy is":* DDED, 4/1/53.

*Eisenhower on Oppenheimer and Rosenbergs:* Lyon, pp. 491–96; Greenstein, p. 169.

**127–128** *Ann Whitman on anticommunist issue:* Ann Whitman Diary, 11/2/53, DDEL.

**128** *"I have just one purpose":* James Hagerty Diary, 12/7/54, DDEL.

**130** *"Eleven years ago":* DDEPP, 7/16/55.

**130–134** *Eisenhower and Khrushchev at Geneva:* James Hagerty oral history, DDEL.

**134** *Khrushchev and Bulganin on Germans and Eastern Europe:* Ambrose, *Eisenhower: The President,* pp. 263–64.

*Eisenhower and Khrushchev on Open Skies:* Charles Bohlen memorandum of conversation, 7/21/55, DDEL; Robert Bowie oral history, Columbia University Oral History project; Author's interview with Andrew Goodpaster, 1/3/83; Eisenhower, *Mandate for Change,* pp. 521–22.

*Bulganin to Eisenhower before leaving Geneva:* Sherman Adams, *Firsthand Report* (Harper & Brothers, 1961), p. 179.

*Macmillan on "no war":* Donald Neff, *Warriors at Suez* (Simon & Schuster, 1981), p. 148.

*Bulganin letter to Eisenhower after summit:* Bulganin to Eisenhower, 8/9/55, DDEL.

**135** *Snyder on Eisenhower's heart attack:* Howard Snyder Papers, draft manuscript, "Heart attack," 12/7/65, DDEL.

*"I never told Mamie," Nixon's reaction to heart attack:* Richard Nixon, *RN* (Grosset, 1978), p. 166.

**138** *Snyder on Eisenhower's complaints about therapy:* Howard Snyder Papers, "Heart attack," 12/7/65.

*"Just what do you think":* Eisenhower to Hazlett, 1/23/56, DDEL.

*British diplomat's exchange with London:* M.C.G. Man dispatch to London, 2/7/56, British Foreign Office Archives, Public Record Office, London.

*Eisenhower to Hauge on second term:* Ann Whitman Diary, 5/25/55.

*"The Republican party must be known":* DDED, 11/20/54.

**140** *"What the failing health":* Eisenhower to Hazlett, 1/23/56, DDEL.

*"I just hate to turn":* James Hagerty Diary, 12/14/55, DDEL.

*Hagerty on Eisenhower's second-term decision:* Hughes, p. 176.

*Eisenhower on Nixon's growth:* Hughes, p. 173.

*Eisenhower suggestion of Pentagon to Nixon:* Nixon, *RN*, p. 167.

**140–141** *Hall-Eisenhower conversation:* Ewald, pp. 185–87.

**141** *Eisenhower on Nixon charting own course:* DDEPP, 3/7/56.

*Eisenhower to Hagerty on Nixon's decision to run:* Nixon, *RN*, pp. 172–73.

*Milton Eisenhower on Nixon's insensitivity:* Author's interview, 3/10/83.

*Nixon on Eisenhower as "genial" yet "cold":* Time, 4/2/90.

*"My 'innards' ":* Eisenhower to Hazlett, 7/3/56, DDEL.

**143** *"The best year":* Author's conversation with Stephen Ambrose.

*"The sorriest and weakest":* Ambrose, *Eisenhower: The President*, p. 597.

**146** *"As inaccessible as Tibet":* Eisenhower, *Waging Peace*, p. 89.

*"Those boys are both furious":* Hughes, p. 223.

*"What in the name of God"* and *"I'm just looking":* Hughes, p. 228.

**5. "EMPIRE . . . CRUMBLING"**

**149** *Eisenhower's call for "cooperation":* Burk, p. 159.

*Eisenhower on Brown setting back integration:* Ambrose, *Eisenhower: The President*, p. 191.

*Eisenhower's opposition to "mingling":* Burk, p. 159.

**151** *"We never thought":* Hughes, p. 247.

*"Outer-space basketball":* Adams, p. 415.

*Eisenhower Gallup decline: Ike* (Time-Life, 1969), pp. 110–11.

*"It is not very reassuring":* Time, 10/28/57.

*Nixon and Dulles on stroke:* Lyon, pp. 760–61.

*"I'm not so sure":* Ellis D. Slater, *The Ike I Knew* (Privately published, 1980), p. 171.

*John Eisenhower on 1958 retirement:* Conversation with the author.

**153–156** *Snyder entries:* Howard Snyder Diary, 10/16/58, 12/3/58, 3/4/59, 3/17/59, 4/11/59, 1/4/60, DDEL.

**156** Washington Post on Gaither Report: *Washington Post*, 12/20/57.

*Alsops on Missile Gap: New York Herald Tribune*, 8/1/58.

*"Unconscionable sums":* DDED, 1/22/52.

*"Any person who doesn't"*: Eisenhower to Charles Wilson, 10/20/51, DDEL.

*"God help the nation"*: Michael R. Beschloss, *Mayday* (Harper & Row, 1986), p. 153.

**157** *"Sanctimonious, hypocritical"*: Barry Goldwater, *With No Apologies* (Morrow, 1979), p. 78.

*Eisenhower on ignoring attacks*: Ann Whitman Diary, 5/2/55, DDEL.

**158** *Eisenhower to Krock on "some agreement"*: Arthur Krock Diary, 7/59, Princeton University.

*"What possible future"*: Ambrose, *Eisenhower: The President*, p. 466.

*Time to "draw the line"*: Eisenhower, *Mandate for Change*, p. 466.

*"No reason why they shouldn't"*: Ambrose, *Eisenhower: The President*, p. 239.

*"The time might come"*: Bundy, p. 278.

*"In the U.S.A. there are still"*: Nikita Khrushchev to Eisenhower, 9/7/58, DDEL.

*"A Gilbert and Sullivan war"*: Ambrose, *Eisenhower: The President*, p. 485.

**158–160** *Gromyko on Mao's demand*: Andrei Gromyko, *Memoirs* (Doubleday, 1990), pp. 251–52.

**160** *"Have worked himself"*: Howard Snyder Diary, 9/11/58, DDEL.

*Eisenhower on "worst" year*: Slater, p. 180.

**161** *"In this gamble"*: Eisenhower, *Waging Peace*, pp. 338–39.

*Eisenhower to Mikoyan*: Memorandum of Eisenhower-Mikoyan conversation, 1/17/59, DDEL.

**163** *"Why should our two countries"*: Memorandum of Eisenhower-Kozlov conversation, 7/1/59, DDEL.

*Eisenhower on paying "penalty"*: Eisenhower, *Waging Peace*, p. 407.

*"I have no other purpose"*: Eisenhower to Nikita Khrushchev, 7/29/59, DDEL.

*"Shook me up a bit"*: Nikita S. Khrushchev, *Khrushchev Remembers: The Last Testament* (Bantam reprint, 1976), p. 425.

**167** *"He was very convivial"*: Adams, pp. 454–55.

*"I would like to wish"*: New York Times, 9/28/59.

*Eisenhower's goodwill trips*: Merriman Smith, *A President's Odyssey* (Harper & Brothers, 1961); Eisenhower, *Waging Peace*, pp. 485–539.

*"Determined"* and *"A ray of light"*: Beschloss, p. 7.

*"What a splendid exit"*: Charles de Gaulle, *Memoirs of Hope: Renewal* (Weidenfeld & Nicholson, 1971), pp. 243–44.

**167–168** *"If one of these aircraft"*: Beschloss, p. 233.

**168** *Goodpaster on "possibly lost" U-2*: Beschloss, p. 34.

*Eisenhower approval of cover story*: Beschloss, p. 37.

*"We have the remnants"*: Beschloss, pp. 58–59.

*"The United States renounce"*: John Eisenhower Diary, 5/14/60; John Eisenhower private papers.

**170** *"Lost his sparkle"*: Howard Snyder Diary, 7/16/60, DDEL.

*Eisenhower to Kistiakowsky*: George B. Kistiakowsky, *A Scientist at the White House* (Harvard, 1976), p. 375.

**170–171** *Eisenhower conversation with Krock*: Arthur Krock Diary, 7/7/60, Princeton University.

**171** *"Difficult" to support a platform*: Eisenhower, *Waging Peace*, p. 595; Ambrose, *Eisenhower: The President*, pp. 597–98.

*"Little Boy Blue"*: Herbert S. Parmet, *JFK* (Dial, 1983), p. 72.

*Slater on Kennedys*: Slater, p. 229.

*"A dangerous man . . . the next thing"*: Parmet, p. 72.

*"If you give me a week"*: DDEPP, 8/24/60.

"Bizarre cardiac reaction": Howard Snyder Diary, 10/17/60, DDEL.

173 "A prolonged conference": Howard Snyder Diary, 10/31/60, DDEL.

"Mamie was plugging": Howard Snyder Diary, 10/28/60, DDEL.

"I know what he wants" and "Ike must never know": Nixon, RN, pp. 222–23.

177 Eisenhower on other time life not worth living: Howard Snyder Diary, 11/12/60, DDEL.

Eisenhower's upset at Nixon's defeat: Slater, pp. 230–31; John S. D. Eisenhower, Strictly Personal (Doubleday, 1974), pp. 285–86; Eisenhower, Waging Peace, p. 602.

"Dick never asked": Slater, p. 230.

"It's like being": Ambrose, Eisenhower: The President, p. 616.

"We have a new genius": Ambrose, Eisenhower: The President, p. 606.

"What happened to all those fine young people": Adams, p. 453.

"I'm going to insist": Slater, p. 231.

Eisenhower anger at Dillon appointment: Ambrose, Eisenhower: The President, p. 606.

Eisenhower on Kennedy "warmth": John Eisenhower, Strictly Personal, p. 286.

Eisenhower on Kennedy visit: DDED, 12/6/60.

177–178 Eisenhower worry about Kennedy attitude toward Presidency: Eisenhower interview by Malcolm Moos, 1966, DDEL.

178 Eisenhower to Dulles on invasion: Peter Wyden, Bay of Pigs (Simon & Schuster, 1979), p. 31.

Farewell Address: DDEPP, 1/17/61.

"Military-industrial-Congressional": Author's interview with Andrew Goodpaster, 6/21/88.

"Insidious penetration: DDEPP, 1/18/61.

"Eerie. . . . Dad spent": John Eisenhower, Strictly Personal, p. 287.

"Look at Ike": Arthur M. Schlesinger, Jr., A Thousand Days (Houghton, 1965), p. 2.

"Choked up a bit": John Eisenhower, Strictly Personal, p. 287.

180 "He was fascinated": Robert Kennedy oral history, John F. Kennedy Library, Boston.

"Fantastic discovery" and "And so we came": Eisenhower, Waging Peace, pp. 618–19.

## 6. "REMAINDER OF OUR LIVES"

185 "He and Mamie": Howard Snyder Diary, 1/20/61, DDEL.

"Within fifteen minutes": Howard Snyder Diary, 1/23/61, 1/24/61, DDEL.

186 "This kind of farm . . . a heritage": Arthur Krock Diary, 1/59, Princeton University.

"You go down there": Ewald, p. 316.

Eisenhower-Kennedy talk after Bay of Pigs: Eisenhower memorandum, 4/22/61; Moos interview with Eisenhower, 1966, DDEL.

"Could not have happened": Slater, p. 244.

John Eisenhower suggested statement: Author's interview, 5/4/83.

"Profile in Timidity": DDED, 6/5/61.

"Terribly unhappy": Slater, p. 243.

186–187 Eisenhower on moon program: Eisenhower to Frank Borman in Ambrose, Eisenhower: The President, p. 641.

187 "The absolute right to use": Moos interview, 1966, DDEL.

190 "The angriest I ever saw": Ewald, p. 315.

"You can always tell": Brendon, p. 399.

"The Boy": William Manchester, The Death of a President (Harper & Row, 1967), p. 55.

*"Eisenhower would be getting madder"*: Robert Kennedy oral history, Kennedy Library.

**190–192** *Eisenhower at library dedication*: New York Times, 5/2/62.

**192** *"What we're trying to do"*: New York Times, 3/29/69.

**193** *Kennedy on Schlesinger poll*: Schlesinger, p. 675.

*Eisenhower comments in 1962 campaign*: New York Times, 9/62–10/62.

*"The Bonus Baby"*: Parmet, p. 72.

**195** *"Of course, it was never done"*: Moos interview, 1966, DDEL.

*"Apparently Ike never did anything wrong"*: Schlesinger, p. 674.

**196** *Eisenhower on Kennedy assassination*: Manchester, *The Death of a President*, p. 394.

*Eisenhower-Johnson meeting*: Eisenhower memorandum, 11/23/63, DDEL.

**196–197** *Eisenhower-Truman exchange*: Virgil Pinkley, *Eisenhower Declassified* (Revell, 1979), p. 374.

**197** *"Dime-store New Deal"*: Ewald, p. 320.

*Eisenhower refuses "cabal"*: Theodore H. White, *The Making of the President: 1964* (Atheneum, 1965), p. 146.

*"Sensation-seeking" journalists* and *"Down with . . . Lippmann"*: White, *Making: 1964*, p. 200.

*Slater on "new leaders"*: Slater, p. 257.

**198** *Eisenhower-Goldwater session* and *"just plain dumb"*: Nixon, *RN*, pp. 261–62.

*"Johnson is unreliable"* and *"He's never had any"*: Ambrose, *Eisenhower: The President*, p. 650.

*Johnson to Eisenhower after election*: Ambrose, *Eisenhower: The President*, p. 655.

*Johnson birthday greeting*: Johnson to Eisenhower, 10/14/67, DDEL.

*"Pass the word back to them"*: Eisenhower memorandum, 2/17/65, DDEL.

*"Untie" Westmoreland*: Eisenhower memorandum, 4/9/65, DDEL.

**202** *"The selfish and cowardly"*: Eisenhower to Robert Anderson, 10/23/66, DDEL.

*Eisenhower on "hot pursuit"*: Ambrose, *Eisenhower: The President*, p. 664.

*"If any Republican"*: Lyon, pp. 847–48.

*Eisenhower coronary after reminder that ten years were up*: John Eisenhower, *Strictly Personal*, p. 328.

**203** *Eisenhower as President on burial*: Ann Whitman Diary, 6/24/58, DDEL.

*"Mamie and I thought"*: New York Times, 4/2/69.

*Eisenhower collapse after son's reburial*: John Eisenhower, *Strictly Personal*, pp. 328–29.

*"I could not resist"*: Johnson to Eisenhower, 2/22/68, DDEL.

**205** *Eisenhower fury at Johnson speech*: Ambrose, *Eisenhower: The President*, p. 665.

*"Dick, I don't want"*: Nixon, *RN*, pp. 275–76.

*"Intellect, acuity"*: Nixon, *RN*, p. 307.

**205–208** *Milton Eisenhower on Nixon endorsement*: Author's interview, 3/10/83.

**208** *Nixon on Bush as "comer"*: Richard Nixon, *In the Arena* (Simon & Schuster, 1990), p. 361.

*"Let's win this one"*: New York Times, 8/9/68.

*Eisenhower on being cripple and burden*: New York Times, 3/29/69.

*"I am still hopeful"*: Slater, p. 270.

*"Few moments in my life"*: Nixon, *RN*, pp. 335–36.

*"My heart, though somewhat"*: Ambrose, *Eisenhower: The President*, p. 673.

**210** *"Can an old sinner":* Pinkley, p. 379.

*"Quite anxious to meet":* Eisenhower to Nixon, 12/13/68, DDEL.

*Kissinger on Eisenhower's eyes:* Henry A. Kissinger, *White House Years* (Little, Brown, 1979), p. 43.

*"It's an eerie feeling," "deep feeling,"* and *Eisenhower's death:* John Eisenhower, *Strictly Personal,* pp. 334–37.

*Johnson wish to be unobtrusive, "ideal plowing weather,"* and *burial: New York Times,* 4/1/69–4/3/69.

**213** *"The most beautiful region":* New York Times, 4/2/69.

## 7. FALL AND RISE

**215** *Gallup Poll on most admired man in U.S.:* George H. Gallup, *The Gallup Poll* (Random House, 1972).

*"My Grandad is now":* Nixon, *RN,* p. 293.

*"He was a great soldier": New York Times,* 3/29/69.

**215–216** *"The Americans themselves say":* Beschloss, p. 307.

**216** *"Virtually everything this Administration has done":* Nixon to Christian Herter, 1/13/61, Christian Herter Papers, Harvard University.

*"The darling":* Manchester, *The Death of a President,* p. 16.

**217** *"The anomaly seemed":* Schlesinger, p. 136.

*"The liberal element, since it does":* Nixon, *RN,* p. 293.

*"Lack of knowledge":* Marquis Childs, *Eisenhower: Captive Hero* (Harcourt, 1958), pp. 291, 286.

*"Kooks and hippies":* Ambrose, *Eisenhower: The President,* p. 664.

*Eisenhower as "warmonger":* Author's conversation with Susan Eisenhower.

**218** *Roosevelt on "really liberal party":* James MacGregor Burns, *Roosevelt: The Lion and the Fox* (Harcourt, 1956), pp. 375–80.

*Leuchtenburg on FDR's shadow:* William Leuchtenburg, *The Shadow of FDR* (Cornell, 1982).

**219** *"Boy, I'd like to fight":* Hughes, p. 250.

*"Sense and honesty":* Hughes, p. 194.

*Johnson on abuse by "Harvards":* Doris Kearns, *Lyndon Johnson and the American Dream* (Harper & Row, 1976), pp. 356–57.

*"Well, when you come down":* DDEPP, 1/18/60.

*Eisenhower concern about military reputation:* Author's interview with John Eisenhower, 5/4/83.

*"I think I pretty well":* Steve Neal, "Why We Were Right to Like Ike," *American Heritage,* 12/85.

*Eisenhower stung by Montgomery's claim:* Ambrose, *Eisenhower: The President,* pp. 499–501, 540–41.

*"You Doubleday people":* Ewald, p. 239.

**220** *Morrow on Eisenhower's intervention against him:* E. Frederic Morrow oral history, DDEL.

*Eisenhower on "honest history":* Author's interview with John Eisenhower, 5/4/83.

*"Afterthoughts":* Drafts dated 1963 and 1964, DDEL.

*Kempton on Eisenhower:* "The Underestimated Dwight D. Eisenhower," *Esquire,* 9/67.

**221** *"Prat boy":* Nixon, *RN,* p. 198.

*Griffith on "corporate commonwealth": American Historical Review,* 2/82.

*Greenstein on Eisenhower:* Greenstein, pp. vii–viii, 137–39.

**222** *Ambrose on Eisenhower:* Ambrose, *Eisenhower: The President,* pp. 9, 12, 627.

*1980s poll on Eisenhower: American Heritage,* 12/85.

*Schlesinger on new scholarship:* Arthur M. Schlesinger, Jr., *The Cycles of American History* (Houghton, 1987), pp. 387–405.

**223** *Ford comparison of self and Truman:* Jules Witcover, *Marathon* (Viking, 1977), p. 79.

**223–224** *Reagan on self and Roosevelt:* Leuchtenburg, pp. 209–35.

**224** *Morrow on Eisenhower nostalgia: Time,* 7/28/80.

**225** *Mondale on Reagan lack of knowledge:* Jack Germond and Jules Witcover, *Wake Us When It's Over* (Macmillan, 1985), pp. 5–7.

*Reagan quotations from Eisenhower:* Ronald Reagan, *Public Papers of the Presidents* (Government Printing Office, 1982–1989), 1/14/82, 5/24/82, 6/17/82, 1/11/83, 1/5/83.

*Twenty-fifth anniversary dinner: Washington Post,* 1/30/86.

**225–226** *Comparison of 1960 and 1988: Life,* 9/88; Peter Goldman and Tom Mathews, *The Quest for the Presidency* (Simon & Schuster, 1989), p. 41.

**226** *Bush camp notes Nixon-Eisenhower parallel:* Jack Germond and Jules Witcover, *Whose Broad Stripes and Bright Stars?* (Warner, 1989), p. 371.

*Prescott Bush on Eisenhower list:* Pinkley, p. 153.

*Bush quotations from Eisenhower:* Fitzhugh Green, *George Bush* (Hippocrene, 1989), p. 179.

*Broder on "Eisenhower Lives": Washington Post,* 9/13/89.

**227** *"If an essential policy":* Kenneth W. Thompson, ed., *The Eisenhower Presidency* (University Press of America, 1984), p. 9.

**228** *Copper box:* Ann Whitman File, DDEL; Martin M. Teasley to the author, 11/8/89.

# PHOTOGRAPH CREDITS

# INDEX

253